Obtaining a
Criminal
Pardon
Clear Your Name Legally

Christopher Guly

Self-Counsel Press
(a division of)
International Self-Counsel Press Ltd.
USA　　　Canada

Self-Counsel Press acknowledges the financial support of the Government of Canada through the Canada Book Fund (CBF) for our publishing activities.

Printed in Canada.

First edition: 2015

Library and Archives Canada Cataloguing in Publication

Guly, Christopher, 1961-, author
    Obtaining a criminal pardon : clear your name legally / Christopher Guly.

(Legal series)
Issued in print and electronic formats.
ISBN 978-1-77040-225-6 (pbk.).—ISBN 978-1-77040-988-0 (epub).—ISBN 978-1-77040-989-7 (kindle)

    1. Criminal records--Expungement—Canada. 2. Criminal records—Expungement—United States. 3. Pardon—Canada. 4. Pardon—United States. I. Title. II. Series: Self-Counsel legal series

K5135.G85 2015   345'.077   C2014-908251-7
                                          C2014-908252-5

Self-Counsel Press
(a division of)
International Self-Counsel Press Ltd.

Bellingham, WA   North Vancouver, BC
USA   Canada

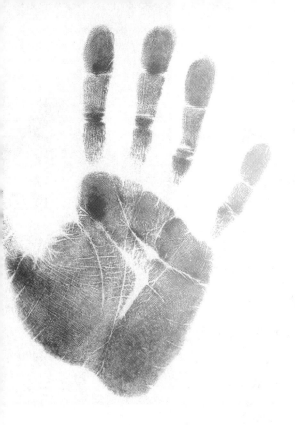

Contents

Table

Notice to Readers

Laws are constantly changing. Every effort is made to keep this publication as current as possible. However, the author, the publisher, and the vendor of this book make no representations or warranties regarding the outcome or the use to which the information in this book is put and are not assuming any liability for any claims, losses, or damages arising out of the use of this book. The reader should not rely on the author or the publisher of this book for any professional advice. Please be sure that you have the most recent edition.

Note: The fees quoted in this book are correct at the date of publication. However, fees are subject to change without notice. For current fees, please check with the court registry or appropriate government office nearest you.

Prices, commissions, fees, and other costs mentioned in the text or shown in samples in this book probably do not reflect real costs where you live. Inflation and other factors, including geography, can cause the costs you might encounter to be much higher or even much lower than those we show. The dollar amounts shown are simply intended as representative examples.

Website links often expire or web pages move, at the time of this book's publication the links were current.

For my mom, Ollie, and my aunt and godmother, Mary,
who always believed in the importance of forgiveness
and the healing power and fresh start that brings;
and my kids, Wolfgang, Monty, Finn, Emma, Henry and Claire,
who were and are living examples of that philosophy.

Acknowledgements

This book would not exist had it not been in the deft editing hands of Tanya Lee Howe; and I would not have written it had there not been the opportunity to work with the maestro, Kirk LaPointe.

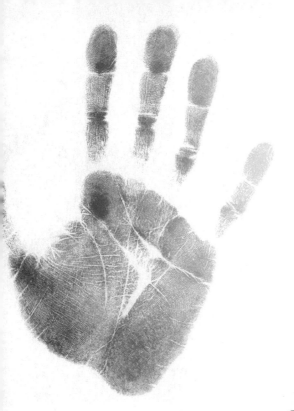

Part 1

Getting a Pardon in the United States

1

Federal Criminal Convictions

Under Article II, section 2, of the US Constitution, the President has the "Power to grant Reprieves and Pardons for offenses against the United States, except in Cases of Impeachment." In other words, the President has the executive power to grant clemency to those who have been convicted of federal criminal offenses adjudicated in the US district courts and in the Superior Court of the District of Columbia.

Executive clemency may take several forms, and applies to the President's constitutional power to exercise leniency toward people who have committed federal crimes, according to the US Department of Justice. These include the following:

- Commutation of sentence.

- Remission of fine or restitution.

- Reprieve.

- Pardon.

A commutation reduces a sentence, either totally or partially, that is being served, but it doesn't change the fact of conviction, imply innocence, or remove civil disabilities that apply to the convicted person as a result of the criminal conviction. To be eligible to apply for commutation of sentence, a person must have reported to prison to begin serving his or her sentence and may not be challenging his or her conviction in the courts.

A commutation may include remission (release) of the financial obligations that are imposed as part of a sentence, such as payment of a fine or restitution. A remission applies only to the part of the financial obligation that has not already been paid.

A person whose petition for commutation of a sentence is denied by the President may reapply one year after the date of the denial. However, a person whose petition for a presidential pardon is denied must wait two years from the date of denial before reapplying. In both cases, you must reapply with a new application form that contains current information in response to all questions.

A pardon is an expression of the President's "forgiveness" and is usually granted in recognition of the applicant's acceptance of responsibility for the crime and established good conduct for a significant period of time after conviction or completion of sentence, according to the US Department of Justice. It is also not a "sign of vindication" signifying innocence, and for that reason, when considering the merits of a pardon petition, pardon officials take into account the petitioner's acceptance of responsibility, remorse, and atonement for the offense.

However, a pardon removes civil disabilities, such as restrictions on the right to vote, hold state or local office, or sit on a jury — imposed because of the conviction for which a pardon is sought, and should lessen the stigma arising from the conviction. It may also be helpful in obtaining licenses, bonding, or employment.

It's important to note that a presidential pardon isn't the only way a person convicted of a federal felony can regain his or her civil rights. Some states have procedures for restoring rights to vote, hold office, or sit on a jury even if a federal felony conviction is involved. If you're thinking about applying for a presidential pardon to restore such rights, you may first wish to contact the clemency authorities in your state of residence to see whether such a procedure exists.

The President decides on most clemency requests unless the following applies:[1]

- Applicant withdraws the petition.

- Applicant repeatedly fails to respond to an Office of the Pardon Attorney request for required information.

- Applicant dies during processing of the application.

- Applicant is released from prison during the processing of a commutation application that seeks only a reduction in the sentence.

Note that a presidential pardon doesn't erase or expunge the record of someone convicted of a crime. However, when a pardon is granted, the Office of the Pardon Attorney notifies the US Probation and Pretrial Services System and other officials in the district of the conviction of the clemency along with the Federal Bureau of Investigation (FBI) to note the pardon in the person's criminal record.

A pardon also doesn't remove the obligation of disclosing a conviction when required to report that information, as the US Department of Justice points out. However, if you obtained a pardon, you may include that information and present the warrant of pardon as evidence.

A person is not eligible to apply for a presidential pardon until a minimum of five years has elapsed since his or her release from any form of confinement imposed on him or her as part of a sentence for the most recent criminal conviction, whether or not that is the conviction for which the individual is seeking the pardon. The Office of the Pardon Attorney usually doesn't accept pardon petitions from people who are on probation, parole, or supervised release.

1. Regain Right to Bear Arms

A presidential pardon is the only way someone convicted of a federal felony offense may regain the right to bear arms. Under US Supreme Court case law interpreting federal firearms laws, a state restoration of civil rights does not remove the federal firearm disability that arises from a federal felony conviction and relief can only be provided through action under federal law. As the US

---

1 "Frequently Asked Questions Concerning Executive Clemency," The United States Department of Justice, accessed March 2015. http://www.justice.gov/pardon/faq.htm

Department of Justice points out, the Attorney General may, under the *Gun Control Act*, grant relief from federal firearms prohibitions "if it is established to his satisfaction that … the applicant will not be likely to act in a manner dangerous to public safety and that the granting of the relief would not be contrary to the public interest."

However, since 1992, the US Congress has prohibited the Bureau of Alcohol, Tobacco, Firearms and Explosives, the agency responsible for processing such requests, from spending any appropriated funds to investigate or act on applications for such relief.

2. Removal or Deportation

Under some — but not all — circumstances, a presidential pardon will eliminate the legal basis for removal or deportation from the US Pursuant to the Rules Governing Petitions for Executive Clemency.

A commutation of sentence has no effect on a person's immigration status and will not prevent removal or deportation from the US.

2.1 Nonresidents

The US Department of Justice's general policy is also not to accept pardon applications from non-US residents given the difficulty in conducting "the type of thorough and exacting investigation into the applicant's personal background and activities"[2] required to determine an applicant's worthiness for a pardon.

3. Posthumous Pardons

The US Department of Justice does not accept posthumous pardons petitions on the basis that many such requests "would likely be based on a claim of manifest injustice, and given that decades have passed since the commission of the offense and the historical record would have to be scoured objectively and comprehensively to investigate such claims. It is the Department's position that the limited resources available to process applications for Presidential pardon are best dedicated to applications submitted by living persons who can truly benefit from a grant of clemency."[3]

---

2 "Pardon Applications Submitted by Non-Residents of the United States," The United States Department of Justice, access March 2015. http://www.justice.gov/pardon/policies.htm#s1
3 "Policy on Posthumous Pardon Applications," The United States Department of Justice, accessed March 2015. http://www.justice.gov/pardon/policies.htm#s1

The US Department of Justice also notes that posthumous-pardon applications are less likely to involve issues generally explored in routine pardon investigations, such as the recent, or ongoing, rehabilitative efforts of a defendant, and would be less likely to benefit from the commonly employed investigative techniques used in the pardon process.

4. Victims

When a clemency request — either in the form of a commutation of a sentence or a pardon of a sentence served — for a conviction of a felony offense involving one or more victims and the Attorney General concludes the investigation of the clemency case warrants contacting the victims of the crime for which clemency is sought of a felony conviction for which there was a victim, and the Attorney General concludes from the information developed in the clemency case that investigation of the clemency case warrants contacting the victim, the Attorney General "shall cause reasonable effort to be made to notify the victim or victims of the crime for which clemency is sought: That a clemency petition has been filed; that the victim may submit comments regarding clemency; and whether the clemency request is granted or denied by the President."[4]

According to the US Department of Justice, in determining whether the victim should be contacted, the Attorney General will consider the following:

- Seriousness of the offense.

- How recent it occurred.

- The nature and extent of the harm to the victim.

- The defendant's overall criminal history and history of violent behavior.

- The likelihood that clemency could be recommended in the case.

A "victim" is defined as someone who has suffered "direct or threatened physical, emotional, or pecuniary harm as a result of the commission of the crime for which clemency is sought (or, in the case of an individual who dies or was rendered incompetent as a direct and proximate result of the commission of the crime

---

4 "Rules Governing Petitions for Executive Clemency," The United States Department of Justice, accessed March 2015. http://www.justice.gov/pardon/clemency.htm

for which clemency is sought, one of the following relatives of the victim [in order of preference]: the spouse; an adult offspring; or a parent);" has filed a request with the Federal Bureau of Prisons to be notified of the offender's release from custody.

5. Federal Misdemeanors

If you've been convicted of a federal misdemeanor, it's unlikely you can obtain a pardon since — as the US Department of Justice explains — most civil disabilities are imposed following a federal conviction of a felony offense. However, you can apply for a waiver of this policy. But in so doing, you must provide "concrete evidence" of a "specific harm or disability suffered that is directly and solely attributable to the misdemeanor federal conviction."[5]

6. Application Process

All requests for executive clemency for federal offenses are directed to the Office of the Pardon Attorney for review, investigation, and preparation of the departmental recommendation to the President — signed off by the Deputy Attorney General — for final disposition of each application. The Office of the Pardon Attorney also prepares the documents the President signs when granting executive clemency and notifies all applicants, in writing, of clemency decisions. (It's important to notify the Office of the Pardon Attorney of any address changes while an application is under consideration.)

The Attorney General reviews every petition and relevant information gathered through the investigation, and then submits a report to the President either recommending or denying clemency. If the President denies a request, the Attorney General notifies the petitioner and closes the case. "Except in cases in which a sentence of death has been imposed, whenever the Attorney General recommends that the President deny a request for clemency and the President does not disapprove or take other action with respect to that adverse recommendation within 30 days after the date of its submission to him or her, it shall be presumed that the President concurs in that adverse recommendation of the Attorney General, and the Attorney General shall so advise the petitioner and close the case,"[6] according to the US Department of Justice.

---

5 "Policy on Pardons for Misdemeanor Federal Convictions," The United States Department of Justice, accessed March 2015. http://www.justice.gov/pardon/policies.htm#s1
6 "Rules Governing Petitions for Executive Clemency," The United States Department of Justice, accessed March 2015. http://www.justice.gov/pardon/clemency.htm

When requesting a pardon, you should state the specific purpose and, if applicable, attach any relevant documentary evidence that indicates how a pardon would help you accomplish that purpose, such as the US Department of Justice illustrates, can include citations to applicable provisions of state constitutions, statutes or regulations, or copies of letters from appropriate officials of administrative agencies, professional associations, or licensing authorities.

There is no fee to apply for any form of executive clemency and no need to hire a lawyer. If you have questions regarding the application process, you can contact the Office of the Pardon Attorney by email (USPardon.Attorney@usdoj.gov). If your application is incomplete or doesn't adequately answer the questions, the Office of the Pardon Attorney will contact you by mail and outline what additional information is required.

A public notice is prepared for each case in which the President grants clemency, and the clemency warrant evidencing the grant is treated as a public record. If a third party inquires about a specific, named person, the Office of the Pardon Attorney will confirm whether that person has applied for clemency and whether clemency has been granted or denied. Furthermore, as the result of a ruling by the federal courts of the District of Columbia in *Lardner v. Department of Justice*, 638 F.Supp.2d 14 (D.D.C. 2009),[7] affirmed, *Lardner v. United States Department of Justice*, No. 09-5337, 2010 WL 4366062 (D.C. Cir. Oct. 28, 2010) (unpublished), the Office of the Pardon Attorney is obliged to release existing lists of the names of persons who have been denied executive clemency by the President to anyone who requests such records under the *Freedom of Information Act and Privacy Act*.

Still, the President's power to commute a sentence for a federal offense is an "extraordinary remedy that is very rarely granted," according to the US Department of Justice.

No hearing is held on either a pardon or commutation application by either the Justice Department or the White House; no appeal is available regarding the President's decision to deny a clemency request.

The Office of the Pardon Attorney does not disclose information regarding the nature or results of any investigation regarding a

---

7   *Lardner v. Department of Justice*, United States Court of Appeals, accessed March 2015.
    Lardner v. Department of Justice

particular case, or the exact point in the clemency process at which a particular petition is pending at a given time. Neither the White House nor the US Department of Justice disclose the reasons to grant or deny a petition, although the President may choose to do so in a particular case, typically by issuing a public statement. Documents related to the US Department of Justice's recommendation to the President in a clemency matter are considered confidential and are not available under existing case law interpreting the *US Freedom of Information Act and Privacy Act*. However, the US Attorney General may make available petitions, reports, memoranda, and communications regarding an executive-clemency request if their disclosure is required by law or the "ends of justice," according to the US Department of Justice.

When completing the application for a pardon, you must disclose any additional arrest or charge by any civilian or military law enforcement authority, including any federal, state, local, or foreign authority, whether it occurred before or after the offense for which you are seeking a pardon, according to the US Department of Justice. You should list every violation, including traffic violations that resulted in an arrest or criminal charge, such as driving under the influence. Failure to disclose any such arrest, whether or not it resulted in conviction, may be construed as a falsification of the petition.

You must also list the following:

- All delinquent credit obligations, whether or not you dispute them.

- All civil lawsuits in which you were named as a party, whether as plaintiff or defendant, including bankruptcy proceedings.

- All unpaid tax obligations, whether federal, state, or local.

You may submit explanatory material in connection with any of these matters (such as an agreed method of payment for indebtedness).

The Office of the Pardon Attorney also requires three character affidavits to accompany the petition (a form is provided with the application). If there are more, you should designate the three persons whom you consider to be primary references. However, letters of recommendation may be substituted if they contain the full name, address, and telephone number of the reference, indicate a knowledge of the offense for which you seek a pardon, and bear a notarized signature. Persons related to you by blood or marriage cannot be used as primary character references, according to the US Department of Justice. A letter of recommendation from a public official carries no special weight when the Office of the Pardon Attorney evaluates a clemency application.

In fact, politics is absent from the review process, states the US Department of Justice. You won't be asked to identify your political affiliation and it will not be considered. You also can't choose which President will decide on your request for clemency, and if there's a change in administration while your application is pending, the new President will consider it. However, you are free to withdraw the application at any time and for any reason before the President has made a decision.

Keep in mind the pardon-application process is lengthy and thorough, so be prepared to answer questions about your personal background and activities. The FBI may also conduct a background investigation. You — or a third party — are also free to submit any information you believe is relevant to your clemency request at any time while your application is pending.

Note that a waiver of any portion of the waiting period is rarely granted and then only in the most exceptional circumstances, according to the US Department of Justice. In order to request a waiver, you must complete the pardon application form and submit it with a letter explaining why you believe the waiting period should be waived in your case.

Although the pardon application is available online, its paper form must be signed and submitted by regular mail. Also note that the personal oath (the Authorization for Release of Information) at the end of the application must be notarized along with the three character affidavits in support of the clemency request, and included with the application. "The candor of the applicant is crucial to the pardon process," the US Department of Justice explains, "and the requirement that the application be executed under oath before a notary public is intended to ensure the applicant's understanding of this fact."

Completed applications should be addressed to the President of the United States and sent to:

Pardon Attorney
Department of Justice
1425 New York Avenue, NW
Suite 11000
Washington, DC 20530

You can find the Petition for Pardon after Completion of Sentence on the US Department of Justice's website: http://www. justice.gov/sites/default/files/pardon/legacy/2010/03/26/ pardon_form.pdf. This link is included in the download kit (see last page of this book for instructions).

In determining whether an applicant qualifies for a pardon, the Office of the Pardon Attorney states that it considers the following:

- The applicant's post-conviction conduct, character, and reputation.

- The nature and seriousness of the offense — and when it occurred.

- The applicant's acceptance of responsibility, remorse, and atonement.

- The applicant's criminal record, if applicable.

- Any hardship the applicant may have because of the conviction and need for relief.

- The nature and extent of post-conviction involvement in community service, or charitable or other meritorious activities. Therefore, highlighting any contributions to community can only help your application.

However, if you don't "fully and accurately" complete the application form, it "may be construed as a falsification of the petition," and result in its denial, warns the US Department of Justice. "In addition, the knowing and willful falsification of a document submitted to the government may subject you to criminal punishment, including up to five years' imprisonment and a [US]$250,000 fine."

2

Standards for Considering Pardon Petitions

According to the US Department of Justice, a pardon is granted on the basis of "the petitioner's demonstrated good conduct for a substantial period of time after conviction and service of sentence."[1] Regulations require a petitioner to wait a period of at least five years after conviction or release from confinement (whichever is later) before filing a pardon application. In determining whether a particular petitioner should be recommended for a pardon, the Office of the Pardon Attorney considers the factors in the following sections.

1. Post-Conviction Conduct, Character, and Reputation

An individual's demonstrated ability to lead a responsible and productive life for a significant period after conviction or release from confinement is viewed as strong evidence of rehabilitation and worthiness for pardon.

---

1   "Section 1-2.112 Standards for Considering Pardon Petitions," United States Department of Justice, accessed March 2015. http://www.justice.gov/pardon/petitions.htm

The background investigation customarily conducted by the FBI in pardon cases focuses on the following:

- The petitioner's financial and employment stability.
- The petitioner's responsibility toward family.
- The petitioner's reputation in the community.
- The petitioner's participation in community service.
- The petitioner's charitable or other meritorious activities.
- The petitioner's military record, if applicable.

The US Department of Justice explains, "In assessing post-conviction accomplishments, each petitioner's life circumstances are considered in their totality: it may not be appropriate or realistic to expect 'extraordinary' post-conviction achievements from individuals who are less fortunately situated in terms of cultural, educational, or economic background."

2. Seriousness and Relative Recentness of the Offense

When an offense is very serious, such as a violent crime, major drug trafficking, breach of public trust, or white-collar fraud involving substantial sums of money, a suitable length of time should have elapsed in order to avoid "denigrating the seriousness of the offense or undermining the deterrent effect of the conviction," says the US Department of Justice. "In the case of a prominent individual or notorious crime, the likely effect of a pardon on law enforcement interests or upon the general public should be taken into account." Victim impact may also be a relevant consideration.

When an offense is very old and relatively minor, "the equities may weigh more heavily in favor of forgiveness," as long as the petitioner is otherwise a suitable candidate for pardon.

3. Acceptance of Responsibility, Remorse, and Atonement

The extent to which a petitioner has accepted responsibility for his or her criminal conduct and made restitution to his or her victims are important considerations, according to the US Department of

Justice. "A petitioner should be genuinely desirous of forgiveness rather than vindication. While the absence of expressions of remorse should not preclude favorable consideration, a petitioner's attempt to minimize or rationalize culpability does not advance the case for pardon." Therefore, statements made in mitigation such as "everybody was doing it" or "I didn't realize it was illegal," should be judged in context. The US Department of Justice cautions that anyone seeking a pardon on grounds of innocence or miscarriage of justice bears a "formidable burden of persuasion."

4. Need for Relief

The reason for seeking a pardon is important since a felony conviction may result in a wide variety of legal disabilities under state or federal law, some of which can provide persuasive grounds for recommending a pardon, as the US Department of Justice points out. "For example, a specific employment-related need for pardon, such as removal of a bar to licensure or bonding, may make an otherwise marginal case sufficiently compelling to warrant a grant in aid of the individual's continuing rehabilitation. On the other hand, the absence of a specific need should not be held against an otherwise deserving applicant, who may understandably be motivated solely by a strong personal desire for a sign of forgiveness."

5. Official Recommendations and Reports

The comments and recommendations of "concerned and knowledgeable officials," particularly the US Attorney whose office prosecuted the case and the sentencing judge, are carefully considered, according to the US Department of Justice. Any likely impact of favorable action in the district or nationally, especially on current law-enforcement priorities, will always be relevant to the President's decision and can play an important role in "defining and furthering the rehabilitative goals of the criminal justice system."

The role of the US Attorney is discussed in more detail in Chapter 4.

6. Effect of a Pardon

The US Department of Justice explains that while a presidential pardon will restore various rights lost as a result of the pardoned offense and should lessen to some extent the stigma arising from a conviction, it will not erase or expunge the record of your conviction. "Therefore, even if you are granted a pardon, you must still disclose your conviction on any form where such information is required, although you may also disclose the fact that you received a pardon."

It notes that "most civil disabilities attendant upon a federal felony conviction, such as loss of the right to vote and hold state public office, are imposed by state rather than federal law, and also may be removed by state action."[2] Consult the appropriate authorities in the state of your residence regarding the procedures for restoring your state civil rights.

---

2   "Effect of a Pardon," United States Department of Justice, accessed March 2015. http://www.justice.
gov/pardon/pardon-information-and-instructions

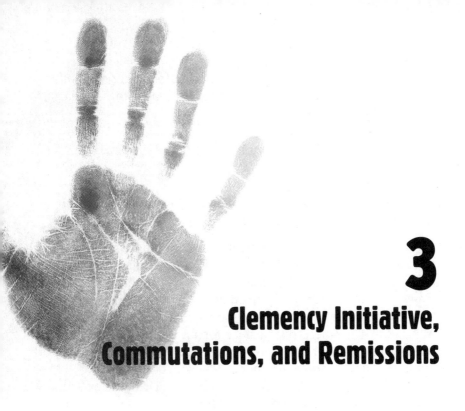

3
Clemency Initiative, Commutations, and Remissions

Pardons are not the only way in which someone with a criminal record can seek some form of relief from a conviction. The President also has the power to reduce a sentence or fine imposed — a form of presidential clemency that provides leniency without implying innocence or extending forgiveness as expressed in a pardon.

1. New Clemency Initiative

On April 23, 2014, US Deputy Attorney General James M. Cole, whose office is responsible for the Office of the Pardon Attorney, announced an initiative to encourage qualified federal inmates to petition having their sentences commuted, or reduced, by the President. Under the initiative, the US Department of Justice will prioritize clemency applications from inmates who meet all of the following criteria:

1. They are currently serving a federal sentence in prison and likely would have received a substantially lower sentence if convicted of the same offense(s) today.

2. They are nonviolent, low-level offenders without significant ties to large-scale criminal organizations, gangs, or cartels.

3. They have served at least ten years of their prison sentence.

4. They do not have a significant criminal history.

5. They have demonstrated good conduct in prison.

6. They have no history of violence prior to or during their current term of imprisonment.

The Office of the Pardon Attorney is working with the Federal Bureau of Prisons to facilitate this initiative. Inmates who appear to meet the six criteria listed above will be offered the assistance of an experienced pro bono attorney through the Clemency Project 2014 in preparing their applications for clemency. The Clemency Project 2014 is solely responsible for any recommendations and determinations of appropriate representation assignments. In addition, the newly formed Clemency Project 2014 is helping to identify appropriate candidates for this initiative. This nongovernment-affiliated organization is composed of the following:

- American Bar Association.

- The National Association of Criminal Defense Lawyers.

- The Federal Defenders.

- The American Civil Liberties Union.

- Families Against Mandatory Minimums.

- Individuals active within those organizations and other lawyers wishing to participate in this volunteer effort.

Public inquiries related to Clemency Project 2014 (or pro bono attorney assignment should be directed to that organization via email (clemencyproject@nacdl.org). For more information about the Clemency Project 2014 go to the website: https://www.clemencyproject2014.org/.

An inmate who applies for clemency pro se (representing one's self) should request Bureau of Prisons staff to submit the petition along with the required documentation from the inmate's central file to the Office of the Pardon Attorney. An inmate who elects to be represented by counsel in filing for commutation should consult with his or her attorney before contacting the office, according to the US Department of Justice.

2. Commutations and Remissions

Inmates of federal prisons can obtain a petition from the warden. All petitions for commutation of sentence should be forwarded to the following address:

> Department of Justice
> 1425 New York Avenue, NW
> Suite 11000
> Washington, DC 20530

On the US Department of Justice's website you will find the Petition for Commutation of Sentence: http://www.justice.gov/sites/default/files/pardon/legacy/2007/06/12/commutation_form.pdf (note there is also a link included in the download kit). There is a sample of this form included at the end of this chapter.

If commutation is granted, the Office of the Pardon Attorney will notify the petitioner through the officer in charge of his or her place of confinement or directly to the petitioner if he or she is on parole, probation, or supervised release.

The completed commutation petition must be typewritten or written in ink and signed by the applicant. Additional pages and documents that "amplify or clarify" answers to any question are allowed.

The petition does not apply to anyone seeking clemency for a state criminal conviction. In that case, you should contact the Governor or other appropriate authorities, such as a state board of pardons and paroles, to determine whether any relief is available under state law.[1]

As previously mentioned, the President's clemency power includes the authority to commute, or reduce, a sentence imposed on conviction of a federal offense, including the authority to remit, or reduce, the amount of a fine or restitution order that has not already been paid. This form of clemency is different from a Petition for Pardon after Completion of Sentence.

---

1 "Commutation Instructions," The United States Department of Justice, accessed March 2015. http://www.justice.gov/pardon/commutation_instructions.htm

Under the current regulations governing petitions for executive clemency, a person may not apply for a full pardon until at least five years after his or her release from incarceration; therefore, the commutation form (see Sample 1 at the end of this chapter) should only be used to seek a reduction of sentence. The waiting period, according to the US Department of Justice, is "designed to afford the petitioner a reasonable period of time in which to demonstrate an ability to lead a responsible, productive, and law-abiding life." However, if a conviction resulted in a sentence that didn't include any prison time, such as community or home confinement, the waiting period begins on the date of sentencing.

Before applying for clemency, the petitioner should have fully satisfied the penalty imposed, including probation, parole, or supervised release. Note that a request for a commutation of a prison sentence generally isn't accepted unless and until a person has begun serving that sentence, or from a person who is currently challenging his or her conviction or sentence through appeal or other court proceeding. In evaluating the merits of a commutation petition, clemency authorities consider the amount of time the petitioner has already served and the availability of other remedies to secure the relief sought, such as parole or judicial action.

The waiting period begins on release from confinement for your most recent conviction, whether or not this is the offense for which a pardon is sought. You can submit a written request for a waiver of this requirement, but a waiver of any portion of the waiting period is rarely granted and only then in the most exceptional circumstances. To request a waiver, you must submit a cover letter explaining why you believe the waiting period should be waived in your case along with the pardon application form.

When completing the form, you should state whether you are seeking reduction of a period of probation, supervised release, or special parole, and explain why this portion of your sentence should be reduced, including the reasons why you believe it would create an unusual hardship for you. In addition, you should explain how requesting the sentencing court or the US Parole Commission to grant early termination of a term of supervision is an inadequate remedy.

Similarly, if you are seeking remission of restitution or fine, you should explain why you believe this portion of your sentence should be reduced, including the reasons why you believe that paying your restitution or fine would present an unusual hardship for you. The Financial Statement of Debtor form (see Sample 2 at the end of this chapter) should be included with your application. You can also find this form online from the Department of Justice: http://www.justice.gov/sites/default/files/pardon/legacy/2012/12/05/financialstatement.individual.pdf.

2.1 Disclosure

You must disclose all additional arrests or charges by any civilian or military law enforcement authority, including any federal, state, local, or foreign authority — whether they occurred before or after the offense for which you are seeking commutation. Every violation (including traffic violations that resulted in an arrest or criminal charge such as driving under the influence) must also be included, along with all convictions (including those that may have been expunged, whether or not they were counted in computing your criminal history category under sentencing guidelines).

Failing to disclose any arrest, whether or not it resulted in a conviction, and every conviction may be considered a false statement, according to the US Department of Justice. In fact, failing to "fully and accurately" complete the application form may be viewed as "a falsification" of the petition and result in its denial. Falsifying a document, knowingly and willfully, may also result in up to five years' imprisonment and a US $250,000 fine.

2.2 Noncitizens

If you are not a US citizen, the commutation of a sentence only shortens the prison sentence and does not result in a change of your immigration status. As the US Department of Justice explains, a full pardon is the only form of executive clemency that might affect a person's immigration status. However, a person serving a prison term is not eligible to apply for that form of relief.

Nevertheless, if a detainer has been lodged against you for deportation or removal, commutation of sentence, if granted, will not prevent your deportation or removal from the US, and may actually hasten the process, according to the US Department of Justice. US Immigration and Customs Enforcement — the Department of Homeland Security agency responsible for decisions regarding a person's immigration status — can determine whether any other relief from deportation or removal is available to you.

2.3 Standards for considering commutations

A commutation of sentence reduces the period of incarceration but has no effect on the underlying conviction and does not necessarily reflect on the fairness of the sentence originally imposed. According to the US Department of Justice, commutation requests are not accepted unless and until a person has begun serving the sentence. They are not usually accepted from anyone challenging a conviction or sentence through an appeal or other court proceeding.

The President may commute a sentence to time served or may reduce a sentence, either merely for the purpose of advancing an inmate's parole eligibility or to achieve the inmate's release after a specified period of time. Commutation may be granted on conditions similar to those imposed regarding parole or supervised release or, in the case of an alien, on condition of deportation.

However, as the US Department of Justice points out, commutation of sentence is an extraordinary remedy that is rarely granted. Appropriate grounds for considering commutation have traditionally included the following:

- Disparity or undue severity of sentence.

- Critical illness.

- Old age.

- Meritorious service rendered to the government by the petitioner, such as cooperation with investigative or prosecutive efforts that have not been adequately rewarded by other official action.

A combination of these and/or other equitable factors may also provide a basis for recommending commutation in the context of a particular case.

Amount of time served and other remedies, such as parole, are also considered. The US Department of Justice can petition the sentencing court through a motion to reward substantial assistance under Rule 35 of the Federal Rules of Criminal Procedure to do the following:

- Correct or reduce a sentence.[2]

- Motion for modification or remission of a fine.[3]

- Request for compassionate relief to reduce a term of imprisonment.[4]

When a petitioner seeks remission of fine or restitution, the ability to pay and any good faith efforts to discharge the obligation are important considerations along with demonstrating "satisfactory" post-conviction conduct, according to the US Department of Justice.

2   "Federal Rules of Criminal Procedure," The Committee on the Judiciary House of Representatives, accessed March 2015. http://www.uscourts.gov/uscourts/rules/criminal-procedure.pdf
3   "18 USC 3573 — Petition of the Government for Modification or Remission," US Government Publishing Office, accessed March 2015. http://www.gpo.gov/fdsys/granule/USCODE-2010-title18/USCODE-2010-title18-partII-chap227-subchapC-sec3573
4   "°3582. Imposition of a Sentence of Imprisonment," Title 18 — Crimes and Criminal Procedure, accessed March 2015. http://www.gpo.gov/fdsys/pkg/USCODE-2013-title18/pdf/USCODE-2013-title18-partII-chap227-subchapD-sec3582.pdf

Sample 1
Petition for Commutation of Sentence

Petition for Commutation of Sentence

Please read the accompanying instructions carefully before completing the application. Type or print the answers in ink. Each question must be answered fully, truthfully and accurately. If the space for any answer is insufficient, you may complete the answer on a separate sheet of paper and attach it to the petition. You may attach any additional documentation that you believe is relevant to your petition. The submission of any material, false information is punishable by up to five years' imprisonment and a fine of not more than $250,000. 18 U.S.C. §§ 1001 and 3571.

Relief sought: *(check one)*

☐ Reduction of Prison Sentence Only
☐ Remission of Fine and/or Restitution Only

☐ Reduction of Prison Sentence and Remission
☑ Other _____

To The President of the United States:

The undersigned petitioner, a Federal prisoner, prays for commutation of sentence and in support thereof states as follows:

1. Full name: _____
    First   Middle   Last

    Reg. No. _____ Social Security No. _____

    Confined in the Federal Institution at _____

    Date and place of birth: _____

    Are you a United States citizen?   ☐ yes ☐ no
    If you are not a U.S. citizen, indicate your country of citizenship

    _____

    Have you ever applied for commutation of sentence before?   ☐ yes ☐ no
    If yes, state the date(s) on which you applied, and the date(s) when you were notified of the final decision on your petition(s).

    _____

Offense(s) For Which Commutation Is Sought

2. I was convicted on a plea of _____ in the United States District Court
    (guilty, not guilty, nolo contendere)

    for the _____ District of _____ of the crime of:
    (Northern, Western, etc.)   (identify state)

United States Department of Justice   *January 2002*
Office of the Pardon Attorney
Washington, D.C. 20530

Sample 1 — Continued

(State specific offense(s); provide citation of statute(s) violated, if known)

_____

_____

_____

I was sentenced on _____, _____ to imprisonment for _____, to pay
               (month/day) _(year)_   _(length of sentence)_

❑ a fine of $ _____, ❑ restitution of $ _____, and to
         (do not include special assessment)

❑ supervised release or ❑ special parole for _____, and/or to probation for

_____. I was _____ years of age when the offense was committed.
(length of sentence)

3.   I began service of the sentence of imprisonment on _____, _____, and I am projected to
                                                     (month/day) _(year)_

be released from confinement on _____, _____.
                                    (month/day) _(year)_

Are you eligible for parole?   ❑ yes ❑ no

If yes, indicate the date when you became eligible for release, and state whether your application for parole was granted or denied

_____

Have you paid in full any fine or restitution imposed on you?   ❑ yes ❑ no

If the fine or restitution has not been paid in full, state the remaining balance.

_____

4.   Did you appeal your conviction or sentence to the United States Court of
Appeals?   ❑ yes ❑ no

Is your appeal concluded?   ❑ yes ❑ no

If yes, indicate whether your conviction or sentence was affirmed or reversed, the date of the decision, and the citation(s) to any published court opinions. Provide copies of any unpublished court decisions concerning such appeals, if they are available to you.

_____

_____

Did you seek review by the Supreme Court?   ❑ yes ❑ no

Is your appeal concluded?   ❑ yes ❑ no

If yes, indicate whether your petition was granted or denied and the date of the decision.

_____

_____

Sample 1 — Continued

Have you filed a challenge to your conviction or sentence under 28 U.S.C. § 2255
(habeas corpus)?   ☐ yes☐ no

Is your challenge concluded?   ☐ yes☐ no

*If yes, indicate whether your motion was granted or denied, the date of the decision, and the citation(s) to any
published court opinions, if known. Provide copies of any unpublished court decisions concerning such motions, if
they are available to you. If you have filed more than one post-conviction motion, provide the requested information
for each such motion.*

---

5.   Provide a complete and detailed account of the offense for which you seek commutation,
        including the full extent of your involvement. If you need more space, you may complete
        your answer on a separate sheet of paper and attach it to the petition.

Sample 1 — Continued

Other Criminal Record

6. Aside from the offense for which commutation is sought, have you ever been arrested or taken into custody by any law enforcement authority, or convicted in any court, either as a juvenile or an adult, for any other incident? ☐ yes ☐ no

For each such incident, provide: the date, the nature of charge, the law enforcement authority involved, and the final disposition of the incident. You must list every violation, including traffic violations that resulted arrest or in an criminal charge, such as driving under the influence.

Arrests:

_____

_____

_____

_____

_____

_____

_____

_____

_____

_____

_____

Convictions:

_____

_____

_____

_____

_____

_____

_____

_____

_____

_____

_____

_____

Sample 1 — Continued

Reasons for Seeking Clemency

7. State your reasons for seeking commutation of sentence. If you need more space, you may complete your answer on a separate sheet of paper and attach it to the petition.

_____

_____

_____

_____

_____

_____

_____

_____

_____

_____

_____

_____

_____

_____

_____

_____

_____

_____

_____

_____

_____

_____

_____

_____

_____

_____

_____

_____

_____

_____

_____

_____

_____

_____

_____

Petition for Commutation of Sentence   _Page 5_

Sample 1 — Continued

Certification and Personal Oath

I hereby certify that all answers to the above questions and all statement contained herein are true and correct to the best of my knowledge, information, and belief. I understand that any intentional misstatements of material facts contained in this application form may cause adverse action on my petition for executive clemency and may subject me to criminal prosecution.

Respectfully submitted this _____ day of _____, _____.
                                              (month)   *(year)*

_____
Signature of Petitioner

Sample 2
Financial Statement of Debtor

U.S. Department of Justice

Financial Statement of Debtor
*(Submitted for Government Action on
Claims Due the United States)*
(NOTE: Use additional sheets where space on this form
is insufficient or continue on reverse side of pages.)

Authority for the solicitation of the requested information is one or more of the following: 5 U.S.C. 301, 901 (see Note, Executive Order 6166, June 10, 1933); 28 U.S.C. 501, *et seq.*; U.S. 31 U.S.C. 951, *et seq.*; 44 U.S.C. 3101; 4 CFR 101, *et seq.*; 28 CFR 0.160, 0.171 and Appendix to Subpart Y.

The principal purpose for gathering this information is to evaluate your capacity to pay the Government's claim or judgment against you. Routine uses of the information are established in the following U.S. Department of Justice Case File Systems published in Vol. 42 of the Federal Register: Justice/CIV-001 at page 53321; Justice/TAX-001 at page 15347; Justice/USA-005 at pages 53406-53407; Justice/USA-007 at pages 53408-53410, Justice/CRIM-016 at page 12774. Disclosure of the information is voluntary. If the requested information is not furnished, the U.S. Department of Justice has the right to such disclosure of the information by legal methods.

Your Social Security account number is helpful for identification, but you are not required to indicate it if you do not desire to do so.

1. Name *(debtor)*	2. Birth Date *(mo. day, yr.)*	3. Social Security No.

4. Home Address	5. Phone No.

6. Name of Spouse *(give address if different from yours)*	7. Date of Birth *(mo. day, year)*

Debtor Employment Data

8. Occupation	9. How Long in Present Employment?

10. Present Employer's Name	Address	Phone No.

11. Other Employment—Within Last Three Years

Employer's Name	Address	Phone No.	Employment Dates

12. Present Monthly Income

Salary or Wages $ _____ Commissions $ _____ Other *(state source)* $ _____ Total $ _____

Spouse's Employment Data

13. Occupation	14. How Long in Present Employment?

15. Spouse's Present Employer's Name	Address	Phone No.

16. Other Employment—Within Last Three Years

Employer's Name	Address	Phone No.	Employment Dates

17. Present Monthly Income

Salary or Wages $ _____ Commissions $ _____ Other *(state source)* $ _____ Total $ _____

Dependents

18. Total Number	Relationship	Age	Relationship	Age	Relationship	Age	19. Total Monthly Income of Dependents *(except spouse)* $ _____

FORM OBD-500
SEP. 82
(PG. 1 OF 4)

Sample 2 — Continued

Financial Data

20. For What Period Did You Last File a Federal Income Tax Return	21. Where Filed	22. Amount of Gross Income Reported

23. Fixed Monthly Expenses

Rent	Food	Utilities	Interest
Debt Repayments *(Including installments)*	Other *(specify)*		
Total Fixed Monthly Charges			

24. Loans Payable

Owed To	Purpose & Date of Loan	Original Amount	Present Balance

25. Assets and Liabilities

Assets	*(Fair market value)*	Liabilities	
Cash	$ _____	Bills Owed *(grocery, doctor, lawyer, etc.)*	$ _____
Checking Accounts *(show location)*		Installment Debt *(car, furniture, clothing, etc.)*	_____
		Taxes Owed	
Savings Accounts *(show location)*		Income Other *(itemize)*	_____
Motor Vehicles		Loans Payable *(to banks, finance Co. etc.)*	
Year Make/License No.		Judgments You Owe	
		Real Estate Mortgages	
Debts Owed to You *(give name of debtor)*		Other Debts *(itemize)*	
Judgments Owed to You			
Stocks, Bonds and Other Securities *(itemize)*			
Household Furniture and Goods			
Items Used In Trade or Business			
Other Personal Property *(itemize)*			
Real Estate			
Total Assets $ _____		Total Liabilities $ _____	

(PG. 2 OF 4)

Sample 2 — Continued

26. Real Estate Owned

Address	How Owned (jointly, individually, etc.)	Date Acquired	Cost	Unpaid Amount of Mortgage

27. Real Estate Being Purchased Under Contract

Address		Name of Seller	
Contract Price	Principal Amount Still Owing	Next Cash Payment Due (date)	Amount (of next payment due)

28. Life Insurance Policies

Company	Face Amount	Cash Surrender Value	Outstanding Loans

29. All Real and Personal Property Owned by Spouse and Dependents Valued in Excess of $200 (List each item separately)

30. All Transfers of Property Including Cash (by loan, gift, sale, etc.) That You Have Made Within the Last Three Years (items of $300 or over)

Date	Amount	Property Transferred	To Whom

31. Are You a Party In Any Law Suit Now Pending?　　　○ Yes, Give Details Below　　○ No

32. Are You a Trustee, Executor, or Administrator?　　　○ Yes, Give Details Below　　○ No

33. Is Anyone Holding any Moneys on Your Behalf?　　　○ Yes, Give Details Below　　○ No

Sample 2 — Continued

34. Is There Any Likelihood You Will Receive an Inheritance?   ◯ Yes, From Whom?   ◯ No

_____

_____

_____

35. Do You Receive, or Under any Circumstances, Expect to Receive Benefits, From any Established Trust, From a Claim for Compensation or Damages, or From a Contingent or Future Interest In Property of any Kind?

◯ Yes, Explain Below   ◯ No

_____

_____

_____

_____

With knowledge of the penalties for false statements provided by 18 United States Code 1001 *(S10,000 fine and/or five years imprisonment)* and with knowledge that this financial statement is submitted by me to affect action by the U.S. Department of Justice, I certify that I believe the above statement is true and that it is a complete statement of all my income and assets, real and personal, whether held in my name or by any other.

_____   _____
Date   Signature

(PG. 4 OF 4)

4
Role of the US Attorney

Official recommendations from officials involved in the case, such as the US Attorney or federal prosecutor for the district of conviction and the sentencing judge, are considered. The Pardon Attorney routinely requests the federal prosecutor to provide comments and recommendations on clemency cases "that appear to have some merit," as well as on cases that "raise issues of fact" that the federal prosecutor may be able to provide information.[1]

Sometimes, the US Attorney in the district in which a petitioner resides may also be contacted. In cases in which the petitioner seeks clemency based on cooperation with the government, the Pardon Attorney may seek views from the federal prosecutor in the districts in which the petitioner cooperated, if different from the district of conviction.

As the US Department of Justice explains, the US Attorney's input is important in providing factual information and perspectives about the offense of conviction that may not be reflected in the presentence or background investigation reports or other sources, such as the following:

---

1 "Standards for Consideration of Clemency Petitioners," The United States Department of Justice, accessed March 2015. http://www.justice.gov/pardon/petitions.htm

- Extent of the petitioner's wrongdoing and the attendant circumstances.

- The amount of money involved or losses sustained.

- The petitioner's involvement in other criminal activity.

- The petitioner's reputation in the community.

- The victim impact of the petitioner's crime, when appropriate.

Occasionally, the Pardon Attorney may request information from prosecution records that may not be readily available from other sources.

Generally in clemency cases, "the correctness of the underlying conviction is assumed, and the question of guilt or innocence is not generally at issue," says the US Department of Justice. "However, if a petitioner refuses to accept guilt, minimizes culpability, or raises a claim of innocence or miscarriage of justice, the United States Attorney should address these issues."

In cases involving a pardon after completion of sentence, the federal prosecutor is expected to comment on the petitioner's post-conviction rehabilitation, "particularly any actions that may evidence a desire to atone for the offense," according to the US Department of Justice. "Similarly, in commutation cases, comments may be sought on developments after sentencing that are relevant to the merits of a petitioner's request for mercy."

In pardon cases, the Pardon Attorney will forward copies of the pardon petition and relevant investigative reports to the US Attorney, which are returned with a response. In cases involving requests for other forms of executive clemency, such as commutation of sentence or remission of fine, copies of the clemency petition and such related records as may be useful as presentence report, judgment of conviction, prison progress reports, and completed statement of debtor forms are provided.

The Pardon Attorney also routinely asks the US Attorney to solicit the views and recommendation of the sentencing judge, according to the US Department of Justice. If the sentencing judge is retired, deceased, or otherwise unavailable for comment, the federal prosecutor should so advise. Should the prosecutor decline to contact the sentencing judge, the Pardon Attorney should be advised accordingly so the judge's views may be solicited directly. "Absent an express request for confidentiality, the Pardon Attorney may share the comments of the United States Attorney with the sentencing judge or other concerned officials whose views are solicited," says the US Department of Justice.

The US Attorney may support, oppose, or take no position on a pardon request, and the Pardon Attorney generally requests a response within 30 days and should be advised in the event of an "unusual" delay.

If desired, the official views of the United States Attorney may be supplemented by separate reports from present or former officials involved in the prosecution of the case, the US Department of Justice explains. The US Attorney may submit a recommendation for or against clemency even if the Pardon Attorney has not yet solicited comments from the district. The Pardon Attorney informs the United States Attorney of the final disposition of any clemency application on which he or she has commented.

5

Pardons for Vietnam War Draft Dodgers and Military Offenses

Arguably, the Vietnam War divided Americans more than any military conflict since the Civil War. Hundreds of thousands of men refused to serve in Vietnam, with as a many as 26,000 draft dodgers coming to Canada between 1965 and 1975, when the Vietnam War ended.[1] More than 200,000 men were formally accused of violating the American draft law. However, Democratic presidential candidate Jimmy Carter wanted to put the Vietnam War in the past and offered to pardon anyone who evaded the draft.[2]

1. Pardons for Vietnam Veterans

In his first day in office on January 21, 1977, President Carter fulfilled his campaign promise and granted pardons to hundreds of thousands of draft dodgers who avoided service during the Vietnam War between August 4, 1964, and March 28, 1973, and

---

1 "The Re-writing of History: The Misuse of the Draft 'Dodger' Myth Against Iraq War Resisters in Canada," ActiveHistory.ca, accessed March 2015. http://activehistory.ca/papers/history-papers-12/#11
2 "1977: President Carter Pardons Draft Dodgers," History, accessed March 2015. http://www.history.com/this-day-in-history/president-carter-pardons-draft-dodgers

violated the *Military Selective Service Act*.[3] However, President Carter's Proclamation 4483 applies only to civilians and not members of the armed forces convicted for a violation of military law during that period who can apply for a presidential pardon under the regular procedure.[4] The Carter Proclamation also doesn't apply to *Military Selective Service Act* violations involving force or violence, or to offenses committed by agents, officers, or employees of the Military Selective Service system regarding duties or responsibilities arising out of their employment.

If you believe you qualify for a Carter pardon, you must submit an application along with documentation that includes the charging document — the indictment or criminal information outlining the factual basis of the offense along with the judgment of conviction or the court docket sheet stating the sentencing date and the sentence imposed for the criminal charge of which you were convicted. Should you not have the documents from your prosecution, they may be available at National Archives (www.archives.gov). However, if you cannot locate this information, the Office of the Pardon Attorney states that it will not be able to proceed with an application. Furthermore, the agency may also verify any documentation you provide with the US Attorney for the district in which you were convicted.

If the Office of the Pardon Attorney concludes the Carter pardon applies to your conviction, you will receive a certificate stating you have been pardoned. The FBI will also be notified to make the appropriate notation in its records.

2. Pardon for a Military Offense

If you are requesting pardon of a court-martial conviction only, you should submit your completed petition directly to the Secretary of the military department that had original jurisdiction in your case, and include all pertinent information concerning your court-martial trial and conviction.[5] The addresses for submitting a request for a pardon of a court-martial conviction are as follows:

---

3 "Proclamation 4483: Granting Pardon for Violations of the *Selective Service Act*," The United States Department of Justice, accessed March 2015. http://www.justice.gov/pardon/carter_proclamation.htm
4 "Vietnam War Era Pardon Instructions," The United States Department of Justice, accessed March 2015. http://www.justice.gov/pardon/carter_instructions.htm
5 "Pardon Information and Instructions," The United States Department of Justice, accessed March 2015. http://www.justice.gov/pardon/pardon_instructions.htm

US Army
Secretary of the Army
Department of the Army
ATTN: OTJAG-CLD
Pentagon
Washington, DC 20310

US Navy and US Marine Corps
Office of the Judge Advocate General
Criminal Law Division (Code 20)
1254 Charles Morris Street SE, Suite B01
Washington Navy Yard, DC 20374

US Air Force
Secretary of the Air Force
Attention: AFLOA/JAJR
1500 West Perimeter Road, Suite 1170
Joint Base Andrews Naval Air Facility, MD 20762

As the US Department of Justice explains, "pardon of a military offense will not change the character of a military discharge. An upgrade or other change to a military discharge may only be accomplished by action of the appropriate military authorities." You can apply for a review of a military discharge by writing to the appropriate military branch:

US Army
Army Review Boards Agency
1901 South Bell Street
Arlington, Virginia 22202-4508

US Navy and US Marine Corps
Secretary of the Navy
Naval Council of Personnel Records
702 Kennon Street, SE, Suite 309
Washington Navy Yard, DC 20374-5023

US Air Force
Air Force Review Boards Agency
SAS/MRBR
550C Street West, Suite 40
Randolph Air Force Base, Texas 78150-4742

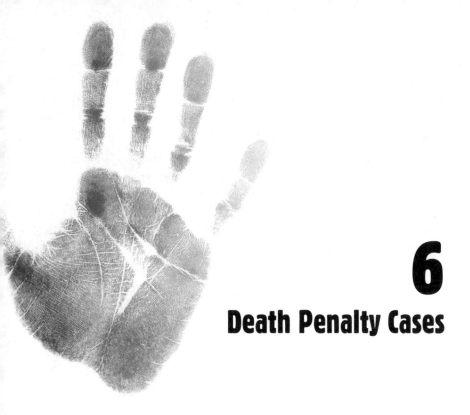

6
Death Penalty Cases

Anyone convicted of a crime carrying a death sentence imposed by a US district court can request clemency in the form of reprieve or commutation — either personally or by the individual's attorney acting with the person's written and signed authorization. However, no such petition should be filed before proceedings on the petitioner's appeal of the judgment of conviction and first petition under 28 US Code ° 2255 (in which a prisoner seeks release from custody on several grounds, including that the sentence was unconstitutional or the court had no jurisdiction to impose the sentence) have concluded.[1]

A prisoner on death row should file a petition for commutation of sentence no later than 30 days after receiving notification from the Bureau of Prisons of the scheduled date of execution. All supporting documents should filed no later than 15 days after the petition has been submitted, otherwise they may not be considered.[2]

When the clemency petition is filed, the petitioner's lawyer may request to make an oral presentation to the Office of the

---

1   "28 US Code ° 2255 — Federal Custody; Remedies on Motion Attacking Sentence," Cornell University Law School, accessed March 2015. http://www.law.cornell.edu/uscode/text/28/2255
2   "Rules Governing Petitions for Executive Clemency," The United States Department of Justice, accessed March 2015. http://www.justice.gov/pardon/clemency.htm

Pardon Attorney in support of the application. The family or families of any victim of an offense for which the petitioner was sentenced to death may, with the assistance of the prosecuting office, also request to appear before the Office of the Pardon Attorney.

Note that clemency proceedings may be suspended if a court orders a stay of execution for any reason other than to allow completion of the clemency proceeding. As well, only one request for commutation of a death sentence will be processed to completion, "absent a clear showing of exceptional circumstances," according to the US Department of Justice.

7

History of Presidential Pardons

All but two Presidents (President William Henry Harrison and President James Garfield) have issued pardons beginning with President George Washington who pardoned, commuted, or rescinded convictions of 16 people, including two convicted of treason during a tax protest known as the Whisky Rebellion.[1] Washington's successors followed suit in issuing often unique presidential pardons.

In terms of quantity, President Jimmy Carter still tops the list with his pardon of Vietnam draft dodgers, of which there were more than 200,000. President Carter also pardoned Peter Yarrow, a member of the folk trio, Peter, Paul, and Mary, who spent three months in prison following a 1970 conviction of taking "improper liberties" with a 14-year-old fan.

In 1974, President Gerald Ford, granted a full and unconditional pardon to his predecessor, President Richard Nixon, for any crimes he may have committed during his presidency as a way, President Ford said, for the nation to move on from the Watergate scandal that forced President Nixon to leave office.

---

1   "On the Chisholm Trail," Historically Speaking — Weekly Column by David Christy, accessed March 2015. http://davidchristyhistoricallyspeaking.blogspot.ca/

President Nixon also handed out pardons to Teamsters' boss Jimmy Hoffa, who was serving a 15-year prison sentence for fraud and jury tampering, and to William Calley, a US Army officer, convicted of killing 22 unarmed civilians in the My Lai Massacre during the Vietnam War.

Among the 393 pardons President Ronald Reagan issued was to New York Yankees' owner George Steinbrenner, who in 1974 was fined $15,000 for making illegal contributions to President Nixon's re-election campaign. President Reagan's vice-president, George H.W. Bush, who succeeded him as the 41st US President, only granted 74 pardons during his four years in office. But six recipients of that executive clemency drew outrage from some quarters. Just a month before leaving office, President Bush pardoned President Reagan's Defense Secretary, Caspar Weinberger, and five others for their involvement in the Iran-Contra affair.

Following the American Civil War, President Andrew Johnson granted unconditional amnesty to all Confederate soldiers, including Confederate States of America Vice-President Alexander Stephens, on Christmas Day 1868. Johnson also commuted sentences handed out to Lincoln-assassination conspirators Samuel Arnold, Edmund Spangler, and Samuel Mudd.

President Ulysses S. Grant — the commanding general who led the Union Armies to victory over the Confederacy in the Civil War and later became the 18th US president — "pardoned 1,332 people,"[2] including many Confederate leaders, under the 1872 *Amnesty Act.*

During the Civil War, President Abraham Lincoln pardoned or rescinded the conviction of 343 people, and including 264 members of the Eastern Sioux band during the Dakota War of 1862. Lincoln also pardoned his sister-in-law, Confederate Emilie Todd Helm, and in a whimsical turn, also offered clemency to a soldier doll, "Jack," shot for desertion by his sons, Willie and Tad.[3]

Some presidential pardons had religious overtones such as in 1893, President Benjamin Harrison issued a mass pardon to members of the Church of Latter Day Saints (Mormons) who had engaged in polygamous or plural marriage after the Church president

2 "Pardon Me, Mr. President," Historically Speaking — Weekly Column by David Christy, accessed March 2015. http://davidchristyhistoricallyspeaking.blogspot.ca/2014/11/pardon-me-mr-president.html?q=pardons
3 "Tad Lincoln," Everything Lincoln, accessed March 2015. http://www.everythinglincoln.com/articles/TadLincoln.html

disavowed the practice. A few decades earlier, President James Buchanan pardoned Brigham Young, a former president of the Mormon Church who founded Salt Lake City and served as the first governor of the independent Utah Territory, for his role in leading a militia against US Army troops dispatched to prevent Utah transforming into a theocracy under Young's leadership.[4]

As blogger David Christy has noted on his blog "Historically Speaking" (http://davidchristyhistoricallyspeaking.blogspot.ca/), President William McKinley pardoned Charles Moore, who was indicted on the federal crime of mailing obscene material and convicted after a jury of 12 Christians focused more on his moral crime of blasphemy, given his opposition to religion and the Bible.

Some pardons have been bestowed posthumously. President Gerald Ford restored full citizenship rights to Confederate General Robert E. Lee, and President Jimmy Carter did the same for Confederate President Jefferson Davis.

However, not everyone is keen to receive a presidential pardon. In 1830, President Andrew Jackson pardoned George Wilson, who was sentenced to death for several mail-robbery crimes. Wilson refused the pardon in a case that wound its way to the Supreme Court, which upheld his right to refuse it. Wilson was hanged.

1. Clemency Statistics from the United States Department of Justice

The following Table 1 lists the different types of presidential clemency granted since the turn of the 20th century. When reading it, keep in mind some nuances as defined by the Office of the Pardon Attorney.

Cases in which multiple forms of relief (pardon, commutation, respite, remission) were granted are counted in only one category. Cases in which clemency was granted to someone who did not file an application have been counted as "petitions granted" since at least fiscal year 1990. The number of commutations don't include two reprieves granted between fiscal years 2000 and 2001. Also excluded are individual members of a class of persons granted pardons by presidential proclamation, such as President Gerald Ford's and President Jimmy Carter's clemency toward Vietnam War draft dodgers.

---

4   "7 Famous Presidential Pardons," History, accessed March 2015. http://www.history.com/news/history-lists/7-famous-presidential-pardons

Regarding some terminology, "fiscal year" once covered the period from July 1 to June 30. However, as of 1976, it runs from October 1 to September 30. Meanwhile, "petitions pending" are those applications pending either at the start of a fiscal year or at the time of a new President's inauguration.

Table 1
Clemency Statistics from the United States Department of Justice

President William McKinley

Fiscal Year	Petitions Pending	Petitions Received	Petitions Granted				Petitions Denied	Closed without Presidential Action
			Pardon	Commutation	Respite	Remission		
1900	68	677	129	73	4	14	131	332
1901	45	796	162	50	2	12	117	448

President Theodore Roosevelt

Fiscal Year	Petitions Pending	Petitions Received	Petitions Granted				Petitions Denied	Closed without Presidential Action
			Pardon	Commutation	Respite	Remission		
1902	50	738	92	36	0	6	181	366
1903	107	543	70	57	0	7	131	316
1904	69	585	87	62	2	11	122	278
1905	90	574	109	52	0	4	119	278
1906	76	627	96	52	1	5	124	363
1907	81	523	71	30	4	10	116	272
1908	49	460	53	22	1	8	56	235
1909	134	463	90	52	1	8	79	220

President William H. Taft

Fiscal Year	Petitions Pending	Petitions Received	Petitions Granted				Petitions Denied	Closed without Presidential Action
			Pardon	Commutation	Respite	Remission		
1910	147	645	111	119	1	24	139	290
1911	108	393	82	64	2	14	84	163
1912	92	412	108	78	2	18	55	173
1913	70	661	82	100	10	16	75	324

Table 1 — Continued

President Woodrow Wilson

Fiscal Year	Petitions Pending	Petitions Received	Petitions Granted				Petitions Denied	Closed without Presidential Action
			Pardon	Commutation	Respite	Remission		
1914	124	664	104	116	1	28	102	345
1915	92	662	78	86	12	10	101	309
1916	158	889	116	107	30	16	109	436
1917	233	938	182	96	43	7	31	510
1918	302	934	119	94	29	14	140	640
1919	200	1,115	116	262	19	18	50	576
1920	274	1,028	198	341	57	43	25	440
1921	198	1,224	174	264	35	12	156	578

President Warren Harding

Fiscal Year	Petitions Pending	Petitions Received	Petitions Granted				Petitions Denied	Closed without Presidential Action
			Pardon	Commutation	Respite	Remission		
1922	208	1,144	162	187	28	13	182	536
1923	244	1,317	138	199	20	26	306	758

President Calvin Coolidge

Fiscal Year	Petitions Pending	Petitions Received	Petitions Granted				Petitions Denied	Closed without Presidential Action
			Pardon	Commutation	Respite	Remission		
1924	114	1,515	105	120	11	11	264	897
1925	221	1,568	182	96	0	11	266	1,017
1926	227	1,209	127	96	2	19	241	755
1927	196	949	89	110	2	20	161	633
1928	130	1,261	110	172	4	36	119	706
1929	244	1,544	160	179	0	29	148	1,082

Table 1 — Continued

President Herbert Hoover

Fiscal Year	Petitions Pending	Petitions Received	Petitions Granted				Petitions Denied	Closed without Presidential Action
			Pardon	Commutation	Respite	Remission		
1930	190	1,141	121	85	1	14	129	783
1931	198	1,195	163	114	0	31	113	785
1932	187	1,203	189	137	0	39	115	699
1933	211	1,235	199	69	0	36	60	686

President Franklin D. Roosevelt

Fiscal Year	Petitions Pending	Petitions Received	Petitions Granted				Petitions Denied	Closed without Presidential Action
			Pardon	Commutation	Respite	Remission		
1934	397	1,061	114	53	2	35	192	662
1935	400	1,407	211	36	3	61	184	757
1936	555	944	154	183	4	49	325	455
1937	329	1,080	192	37	3	59	137	653
1938	328	1,287	219	28	0	92	160	797
1939	319	1,215	172	32	0	40	139	729
1940	422	1,293	242	31	0	40	104	791
1941	510	1,367	178	15	0	18	74	910
1942	682	1,272	305	21	0	51	55	599
1943	923	1,019	332	17	0	10	55	748
1944	780	781	424	10	0	10	60	586
1945	471	815	276	25	0	12	29	506

Table 1 — Continued

President Harry S. Truman

Fiscal Year	Petitions Pending	Petitions Received	Petitions Granted			Petitions Denied or Closed without Presidential Action
			Pardon	Commutation	Remission	
1945 (2.5 months)	479	201	98	9	2	133
1946	438	977	279	28	3	570
1947	535	779	308	13	2	483
1948	508	657	178	15	0	411
1949	561	638	178	17	1	313
1950	690	504	400	14	3	338
1951	439	467	189	10	1	228
1952	478	477	192	6	0	214
1953 (6.5 months)	543	330	91	6	1	197
Total (93 months)		5,030	1,913	118	13	2,887

President Dwight D. Eisenhower

Fiscal Year	Petitions Pending	Petitions Received	Petitions Granted			Petitions Denied or Closed without Presidential Action
			Pardon	Commutation	Remission	
1953 (5.5 months)	578	269	6	1	0	159
1954	681	461	55	7	0	348
1955	732	662	59	4	0	684
1956	647	585	192	9	0	568
1957	463	585	232	4	0	443
1958	369	406	98	6	0	302
1959	369	434	117	2	0	286
1960	398	437	149	5	0	244
1961 (6.5 months)	437	261	202	9	0	145
Total (96 months)		4,100	1,110	47	0	3,179

Table 1 — Continued

President John F. Kennedy

Fiscal Year	Petitions Pending	Petitions Received	Petitions Granted			Petitions Denied or Closed without Presidential Action
			Pardon	Commutation	Remission	
1961 (5.5 months)	342	220	24	9	0	121
1962	408	595	166	16	0	315
1963	506	592	133	43	2	233
1964 (4.5 months)	687	342	149	32	1	162
Total (34 months)		1,749	472	100	3	831

President Lyndon B. Johnson

Fiscal Year	Petitions Pending		Petitions Received		Petitions Granted			Petitions Denied or Closed without Presidential Action	
	P	C	P	C	P	C	R	P	C
1964 (7.5 months)	685		579		166	40	0	275	
1965	783		1,008		195	80	0	569	
1966	947		865		364	80	1	726	
1967	532	109	419	444	222	23	0	147	373
1968	582	157	409	340	13	3	0	106	309
1969 (6.5 months)	872	185	278	195	0	0	0	129	196
Total (62 months)			4,537		960	226	1	2,830	

Table 1 — Continued

President Richard. M Nixon

Fiscal Year	Petitions Pending		Petitions Received		Petitions Granted			Petitions Denied or Closed without Presidential Action	
	P	C	P	C	P	C	R	P	C
1969 (5.5 months)	1,021	184	136	115	0	0	0	123	57
1970	1,034	242	337	122	82	14	0	432	266
1971	857	84	266	188	157	16	0	436	212
1972	530	44	346	170	235	18	2	252	158
1973	389	36	323	162	202	4	1	198	143
1974	312	50	291	135	187	8	0	209	128
1975 (1.5 months)	207	49	-	-	0	0	0	0	0
Total (67 months)			1,699	892	863	60	3	1,650	964

President Gerald R. Ford

Fiscal Year	Petitions Pending		Petitions Received		Petitions Granted			Petitions Denied or Closed without Presidential Action	
	P	C	P	C	P	C	R	P	C
1975 (10.5 months)	207	49	351	259	147	5	4	166	159
1976 (15 months)	245	140	502	240	106	11	0	199	243
1977 (3.5 months)	442	126	125	50	129	6	1	70	63
Total (29 months)			978	549	382	22	5	435	465

Table 1 — Continued

President Jimmy Carter

Fiscal Year	Petitions Pending		Petitions Received		Petitions Granted			Petitions Denied		Petitions Closed without Presidential Action	
	P	C	P	C	P	C	R	P	C	P	C
1977 (8.5 months)	368	106	292	271	0	1	0	1	0	118	49
1978	541	327	379	262	162	3	0	307	409	74	46
1979	377	131	436	274	143	10	0	138	123	55	132
1980	477	140	355	168	155	8	3	150	106	161	81
1981 (3.5 months)	366	108	119	71	74	7	0	42	35	11	18
Total (48 months)			1,581	1,046	534	29	3	638	673	419	326

President Ronald Reagan

Fiscal Year	Petitions Pending		Petitions Received		Petitions Granted			Petitions Denied		Petitions Closed without Presidential Action	
	P	C	P	C	P	C	R	P	C	P	C
1981 (8.5 months)	358	119	220	137	2	0	0	0	0	66	87
1982	510	169	283	179	83	3	0	258	123	81	85
1983	371	137	298	149	91	2	0	74	33	96	103
1984	409	147	289	158	37	5	0	99	31	95	101
1985	467	168	256	151	32	3	0	86	18	66	109
1986	540	188	222	140	55	0	0	94	28	65	103
1987	548	197	227	183	23	0	0	115	34	52	110
1988	588	236	236	148	38	0	0	205	43	68	181
1989 (3.5 months)	513	160	68	60	32	0	0	38	8	23	26
Total (96 months)			2,099	1,305	393	13	0	969	318	612	905

Table 1 — Continued

President George H. W. Bush

Fiscal Year	Petitions Pending		Petitions Received		Petitions Granted			Petitions Denied		Petitions Closed without Presidential Action	
	P	C	P	C	P	C	R	P	C	P	C
1989 (8.5 months)	488	186	115	130	9	1	0	122	22	41	112
1990	432	184	206	148	0	0	0	94	22	59	114
1991	485	196	172	146	29	0	0	390	198	62	31
1992	180	109	174	205	0	0	0	45	76	40	31
1993 (3.5 months)	269	207	64	106	36	2	0	25	111	18	8
Total (48 months)			731	735	74	3	0	676	429	220	296

President William J. Clinton

Fiscal Year	Petitions Pending		Petitions Received		Petitions Granted			Petitions Denied		Petitions Closed without Presidential Action	
	P	C	P	C	P	C	R	P	C	P	C
1993 (8.5 months)	260	192	172	526	0	0	0	1	2	33	53
1994	392	656	228	580	0	0	0	175	400	74	136
1995	371	700	209	403	53	3	0	158	258	39	133
1996	330	709	204	308	0	0	0	72	139	23	137
1997	438	736	209	476	0	0	0	69	325	38	123
1998	540	764	201	407	21	0	0	54	126	37	161
1999	628	884	261	748	34	12	2	126	231	36	208
2000	693	1,179	336	1,052	70	6	0	0	790	61	176
2001 (3.5 months)	894	1,259	181	988	218	40	0	0	116	12	32
Total (96 months)			2,001	5,488	396	61	2	655	2,387	353	1,159

Table 1 — Continued

President George W. Bush

Fiscal Year	Petitions Pending		Petitions Received		Petitions Granted			Petitions Denied		Petitions Closed without Presidential Action	
	P	C	P	C	P	C	R	P	C	P	C
2001 (8.5 months)	923	2,063	110	548	0	0	0	0	1	45	277
2002	988	2,332	152	1,096	0	0	0	519	1,466	53	240
2003	565	1,715	172	851	7	0	0	51	819	21	159
2004	659	1,588	235	951	12	2	0	108	632	42	178
2005	733	1,728	252	807	39	0	0	89	411	35	296
2006	822	1,829	254	759	39	0	0	255	779	53	315
2007	729	1,495	334	925	16	2	0	0	0	75	336
2008	972	2,083	555	1,770	44	2	0	513	2,182	107	360
2009 (3.5 months)	864	1,309	434	869	32	5	0	194	1,208	33	62
Total (96 months)			2,498	8,576	189	11	0	1,729	7,498	464	2,223

Table 1 — Continued

President Barack Obama

Fiscal Year	Petitions Pending		Petitions Received		Petitions Granted			Petitions Denied		Petitions Closed without Presidential Action	
	P	C	P	C	P	C	R	P	C	P	C
2009 (8.5 months)	1,040	903	232	1,086	0	0	0	0	0	132	120
2010	1,140	1,869	262	1,902	0	0	0	0	0	117	340
2011	1,285	3,431	331	1,585	17	0	0	872	3,104	84	389
2012	643	1,523	383	1,547	5	1	0	147	689	48	148
2013	826	2,232	303	2,370	17	0	0	314	1,577	44	240
2014	754	2,785	273	6,561	13	9	0	154	1,226	36	222
FY 2015 (3 months)	824	7,889	48	874	12	11	0	142	782	0	51
Total (70.5 months)			1,832	15,925	64	21	0	1,629	7,378	461	1,510

8
State Pardons

The governors of most of the 50 US states have the power to grant pardons or reprieves for offenses committed under state criminal law. In other states, pardons are determined by an agency or an appointed board or to the governor on the advice of a pardon. Nine states have boards of pardons that exclusively grant all state pardons:

- Alabama (Board of Pardons and Paroles).
- Connecticut (Board of Pardons and Paroles).
- Georgia (State Board of Pardons).
- Idaho (Commission of Pardons and Parole).
- Minnesota (Board of Pardons).
- Nebraska (Board of Pardons).
- Nevada (Board of Pardon Commissioners).
- South Carolina (Board of Probation, Parole and Pardon Services).
- Utah (Board of Pardons and Parole).

1. California

The Governor may grant a pardon to anyone who has demonstrated "exemplary behavior" following his or her conviction, according to the California Governor's office.[1] "A pardon will not be granted unless it has been earned," and Gubernatorial Pardons are very rare in California.

Applications will not generally be accepted unless the applicant has been discharged from probation or parole for at least ten years without further criminal activity during that period.

To apply for a pardon, an individual must first obtain a certificate of rehabilitation from the Superior Court in the county where the applicant lives. Those ineligible for the certificate or who reside outside California, must use the Application for Gubernatorial Pardon (http://gov.ca.gov/docs/Application_for_Pardon.pdf).

A Certificate of Rehabilitation is a court order that declares a person convicted of a crime rehabilitated.[2] An application for the certificate can usually be obtained from the court clerk, probation department, or public defender's office. Once a petition is filed, the court may require an investigation by the district attorney and will schedule a hearing. If the court issues a Certificate of Rehabilitation, it is forwarded to the Governor's Office as a pardon application.

A certificate relieves some sex offenders of further duty to register. It is an official document to demonstrate rehabilitation, which can help with finding employment, and serves as an automatic application for a gubernatorial pardon. However, it does *not* do the following:

- Seal or erase the record of conviction (neither does a Governor's pardon or gubernatorial pardon).

- Prevent the offense from being considered as a prior conviction if the person is later convicted of a new offense (neither does a Governor's pardon).

- Restore the right to own or possess firearms.

The Governor's pardon or direct pardon procedure is available to people who are ineligible for a Certificate of Rehabilitation. This

---

1 "Pardons and Commutations," Office of Governor Edmund G. Brown, Jr., accessed March 2015. http://gov.ca.gov/s_pardonsandcommutations.php
2 "How to Apply for a Pardon," State of California Office of Governor Edmund G. Brown, Jr., accessed March 2015. http://gov.ca.gov/docs/How_To_Apply_for_a_Pardon.pdf

procedure is used primarily by people convicted of a crime in California and who now reside outside the state. The direct pardon procedure is also available to people who are not eligible for a Certificate of Rehabilitation because they have been convicted of specified sex offenses or misdemeanor offenses.

A direct or gubernatorial pardon is used mainly by people convicted of a crime in California and who live outside the state, but is also available to those convicted of specific sex offenses or misdemeanors. You can obtain an application for a Gubernatorial Pardon either via the Governor's website (www.gov.ca.gov) or by writing to the following address:

> Governor's Office
> State Capitol
> Attention: Legal Affairs, State Capitol
> Sacramento, CA 95814

As the Governor's Office notes, you should first complete the Application for Executive Clemency (http://gov.ca.gov/docs/Application_for_Executive_Clemency.pdf), and the send a Notice of Intent to Apply for Executive Clemency to the District Attorney in each county in which you were convicted so each District Attorney receives the legally required notice. The District Attorney then acknowledges receipt of the Notice of Intent and forwards it to the Governor's Office. You then return the completed application to the Governor's Office at the address listed above.

Keep in mind the Governor isn't required to act on a pardon application. Once a request for a Certificate of Rehabilitation or direct pardon is received, the Governor's Office forwards it to the Board of Parole Hearings, which may conduct a background investigation involving the District Attorney, law enforcement, and anyone with "relevant" information on the applicant before recommending whether or not a pardon should be granted.

If an applicant has been convicted of more than one felony, the California Supreme Court must recommend granting a pardon before the Governor may do so, as the Governor's Office explains. However, the Governor isn't required to seek a recommendation from this court if only one felony conviction is involved.

The Governor's Office also notes the length of time required to complete the pardon process cannot be predicted.

A Governor's pardon doesn't necessarily prevent deportation but it allows you to do the following:

- Serve on a jury trial.

- Restores your right to bear firearms (upon federal approval, to specified offenders who obtained a Certificate of Rehabilitation if granted a full and unconditional pardon, unless the conviction involved the use of a dangerous weapon).

- Apply for a job as a county probation officer or state parole agent (but not any other peace-officer positions).

- Enables specified sex offenders, still required to register after obtaining a Certificate of Rehabilitation, to no longer register if granted a full and unconditional pardon.

2. New York

A 19-member Board of Parole investigates and advises the New York Governor on pardon applications. The Governor can grant clemency for all state offenses except treason and cases of impeachment, and can impose any conditions, limitations, or restrictions "as he may think proper," according to the State Constitution. Gubernatorial clemency is only granted "under the most compelling circumstances," cautions the New York State Department of Corrections and Community Supervision.[3]

New York State Corrections explains that pardons are only considered if no other administrative or legal remedy is available, such as to set aside a conviction when there is "overwhelming and convincing proof" (e.g., DNA evidence illustrating innocence) unavailable at the time of conviction; to relieve a disability, such as ineligibility to vote, own a gun, or possess a state occupational licenses for first offenders; or to prevent deportation or permit re-entry into the US.

If you apply for a pardon in New York State, you "must demonstrate a specific and compelling need for relief and a substantial period of good citizenship," according to the State's website on clemency.[4]

---

3 "Executive Clemency," NYS Department of Corrections and Community Supervision, accessed March 2015. https://www.parole.ny.gov/clemency.html
4 "Apply for Clemency," New York State, accessed March 2015. http://www.ny.gov/services/apply-clemency

However, absent "exceptional" circumstances, you won't be able to apply for a pardon if other remedies are available, such as a Certificate of Good Conduct or a Certificate of Relief from Disabilities. For more information about these certificates, write to the following address:

New York State Department of Corrections and
    Community Supervision
Executive Clemency Bureau
The Harriman State Campus — Building 2
1220 Washington Avenue
Albany, NY 12226-2050

Or write to the following email address:

PardonsAndCommutations@doccs.ny.gov

You should also send your pardon request to the mailing address and (in scanned form) to the email address listed above.

Your application should include a letter outlining your need for a pardon, along with examples of "rehabilitation" and "positive accomplishments" since your conviction, such as the following:

• Community involvement.

• Education achievements.

• Employment history.

• Volunteer service.

Also required is proof of these accomplishments, such as degrees obtained, certificates of completion, and commendation letters. You can also submit letters of support from family, friends, or community members.

The pardon application should also be accompanied by a certified copy of any judgment or conviction rendered against you at any time during your life.

Sample 3 shows you a New York Pardon Request — Background Information Form. You can also find it online at: https://www.ny.gov/sites/ny.gov/files/atoms/files/pardon_request_form.pdf

Corrections and Community Supervision

ANDREW M. CUOMO
Governor

ANTHONY J. ANNUCCI
Acting Commissioner

THOMAS J. HERZOG
Deputy Commissioner

PARDON REQUEST - BACKGROUND INFORMATION FORM

Please complete this form, to the best of your knowledge, and return to:
NYS Department of Corrections and Community Supervision
Executive Clemency Bureau
The Harriman State Campus – Building 2
1220 Washington Avenue
Albany, NY 12226-2050

Full Name of Applicant:

Current Address:

Phone Number(s):

Alias:

Date of Birth: Year Month Day

Social Security Number:

DIN # NYSID# FBI #

Alien Registration # (for immigration cases):

Whether immigration proceedings are pending and the status:

Conviction(s) - Please note: include only NYS convictions:

Place of Crime(s):

Sentencing Date(s):

Sentence(s) Received:

Reason for Request (attach additional papers or write on back if necessary):

Any other identifying information (attach additional papers or write on back if necessary):

Applicant Signature: _____ Date

The Harriman State Campus, Building 2, 1220 Washington Avenue, Albany, New York 12226-2050

3. Massachusetts Pardon Petition for Mark Wahlberg

In late 2014, Oscar-nominated actor Mark Wahlberg made international headlines when *New England Cable News* revealed he applied for a pardon to the Massachusetts Advisory Board of Pardons regarding an assault he committed on April 8, 1988, at the age of 16.

Wahlberg states in his petition that he tried to steal two cases of alcohol from a man standing outside a convenience store near his family home in Boston and hit the man on the head with a wooden stick. While attempting to avoid police, he punched another man in the face, and in his application, admitted to being under the influence of "alcohol and narcotics."[5]

The United Kingdom's *Daily Mail* newspaper reported that the two men were of Vietnamese origin, and that Hoa (Johnny) Trinh, whom Wahlberg punched in the eye according to a police document filed in court, has forgiven his future movie-star assailant.

Not everyone is as charitable. A petition, launched by the online group 18MillionRising.org that promotes civic engagement among the estimated 18 million Asians and Pacific Islanders in the US, aims to get 25,600 signatures blocking Wahlberg's attempt to secure a pardon since court documents show he yelled racial slurs at his victims and only wants clemency to expand his Wahlburgers hamburger chain into California where he would be unable to obtain a liquor license as a convicted felon.

Wahlberg, who first attained fame as hip-hop artist "Marky Mark" and was born on June 5, 1971, faced several charges from the incident. Although he was a teen at the time of the crime, Wahlberg was tried as an adult, convicted of assault and battery, and spent 45 days in prison.

In his pardon application, Wahlberg expressed remorse "for any lasting damage" he might have caused his victims — and noted that since that time, he has dedicated himself "to becoming a better person and citizen so that [he] can be a role model to [his four] children and other." He said his philanthropic activity, which includes an eponymous youth foundation that he and his brother, James, established in 2001, is not intended "to make people forget

---

5   "The Commonwealth of Massachusetts Pardon Petition for Mark Wahlberg," accessed March 2015. http://media.nbcbayarea.com/documents/wahlberg.pdf

about my past. To the contrary, I want people to remember my past so that I can serve as an example of how lives can be turned around and how people can be redeemed."

Receiving a pardon, "would be a formal recognition that I am not the same person that I was on the night of April 8, 1988," explained Wahlberg, who also noted that it would allow him to obtain such law-enforcement positions as a parole or probation officer. "It would be formal recognition that someone like me can receive *official* public redemption if he devotes himself to personal improvement and a life of good works."

4. Pardon411.com

Detailed information about applying for a pardon in all 50 states is available at Pardon411.com, a site run by the Foundation for Continuing Justice (ContinuingJustice.org), a Santa Ana, California-based nonprofit law firm whose staff attorneys have written the information snapshots or profiles per state.

California lawyer and foundation chairman, Mathew Higbee, is the primary author of Pardon411.com content and recognized as one of the leading authorities on criminal-record clearing in the US. He says that executive pardon power is generally "underused" and when used, is often "abused."

He explains that at the federal level, pardons appear to be granted at the end of a President's term in office and usually have a "strong smell of cronyism" attached to many of them. Meanwhile, the pattern for state-level pardons is inconsistent, according to 2012 data collected by the Foundation for Continuing Justice. For instance, no pardons had been issued in Rhode Island for 50 years, while the pardon process in Wisconsin had been suspended indefinitely.

Pennsylvania Governor Ed Rendell, a Democrat and former mayor and district attorney of Philadelphia, signed more than 1,000 pardons a month before leaving office in 2011, which is twice as many pardons as any of his predecessors.[6] The most common convictions for which Governor Rendell granted pardons involved shoplifting, other forms of theft, and drug offenses. A spokesman from the Governor's office told *The Associated Press* that Governor

6 "Govenor Ed Rendell Grants 1,000+ Pardons, More than Twice any other Pennsylvania Governor," *The Associated Press*, accessed March 2015. http://www.pennlive.com/midstate/index.ssf/2010/12/ gov_ed_rendell_grants_1000_par.html

Rendell's administration received ten times as many applications than there were under the late Democratic Governor Milton Shapp, the previous record holder who issued 475 pardons during his tenure from 1971 to 1979.

Some governors have used their powers to pardon to save prisoners from the death penalty, such as New Mexico's Toney Anaya, a Democrat, who commuted the sentences of five death-row inmates in 1986.

In a more celebrated case George Ryan, the Republican governor of Illinois from 1999 to 2003, declared a moratorium on state executions in 2000 and just before leaving office, commuted the sentences of 167 of death-row inmates and freed four others. However, three years after leaving office, Ryan was convicted of federal corruption charges and spent more than five years in prison. President George W. Bush denied his request for a pardon.

However, as Higbee points out, there is no coherent nationwide policy that aims to provide executive clemeney to people "who deserve to be forgiven and put back in their proper place in society." He explains that part of the problem is that presidents and governors obtain "little gain" in granting pardons, particularly following the spate of controversial pardons Bill Clinton issued before he left office on January 20, 2001.

The controversy wasn't so much over the number of pardons (396) that President Clinton signed. His Democratic presidential predecessor, President Jimmy Carter, issued far more (534), according to the Office of the Pardon Attorney. President Clinton's crime in the court of public opinion was whom he pardoned, according to Higbee. Among the 140 people pardoned on the 42nd President's last day were his former Whitewater real estate business partner, Susan McDougal, who served time for fraud, conspiracy, and civil contempt; and Marc Rich and business partner, Pincus Green, who fled the US rather than face indictments on 65 criminal counts in what was at the time the largest tax-evasion case in American history. In a February 18, 2001, *The New York Times* op-ed, President Clinton defended the latter pardons as being "in the best interests of justice," for several reasons, including the option they could still face civil fines or penalties. (Marc Rich died in 2013 in Switzerland, where he had been a fugitive.)

President Clinton's last act of amnesty also handed pardons to Patty Hearst, the publishing heiress who was kidnapped by and later joined the California-based Symbionese Liberation Army in 1974 in a bank robbery, and Clinton's half-brother, Roger Clinton, who spent a year in prison on a cocaine-distribution conviction.

Higbee says President Clinton's successors (President George W. Bush and President Barack Obama) have been reluctant to grant nearly as many pardons. President Bush issued 189 by the end of his term, while President Obama, as of the end of 2014, only issued 64 out of 1,832 petitions received.[7]

"Few states also want to touch them," says Higbee, who explains that applicants have better odds obtaining a pardon in Pennsylvania or Illinois than they do in California, Florida, or Texas. He adds that 99 percent of criminal convictions in the US occur at the state level.

However, if states are reticent to grant pardons, courts can provide relief for those with a thin criminal record consisting of perhaps one or two convictions at the county level and which resulted in fines rather than a prison term. They can, as Higbee points out, ask a judge to expunge or clear their record.

---

7   "Clemency Statistics," The United States Department of Justice, accessed March 2015. http://www.justice.gov/pardon/statistics.htm

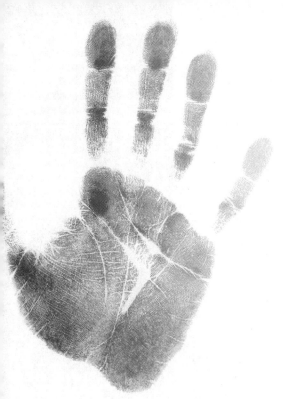

Part 2
Getting a Pardon in Canada

9

Record Suspensions

In Canada, a pardon is now known as a "record suspension" and is granted under the *Criminal Records Act*. There is another form of clemency known as the "royal prerogative of mercy" granted by the Crown in exceptional circumstances (see Chapter 14).

A record suspension allows people who were convicted of a criminal offense, but have completed their sentence and demonstrated they are law-abiding citizens, to have their criminal record set aside, but not erased. If you get a record suspension, barriers are removed to applying for Canadian citizenship, working as a teacher, working in health care or government, getting bonded, adopting children, and often even getting insurance or volunteering. However, a record suspension doesn't guarantee entry or visa privileges to another country.

Suspended records of former sexual offenders are also flagged in the Canadian Police Information Centre (CPIC) database to conduct a vulnerable sector check should someone apply to work or volunteer in such a sector, according to the Parole Board of Canada (PBC), which is the only federal agency responsible for ordering, denying, and revoking record suspensions under the *Criminal Records Act*.

According to the PBC, all conviction-related information is removed from CPIC — the country's national criminal records database — and may not be disclosed without permission from the Minister of Public Safety Canada.

The *Criminal Records Act* applies only to records kept within federal departments and agencies. However, many provincial and municipal law-enforcement agencies cooperate by restricting access to their records once notified that a record suspension has been ordered.

To be eligible to apply for a record suspension, a person must have paid all fines, surcharges, costs, restitution, and compensation orders in full; served all sentences of imprisonment and/or conditional sentences, including parole and statutory release; and satisfied his or her probation order(s).

There is also a waiting period: five years for a summary offense, or a service offense under the *National Defence Act*; and ten years for an indictable offense (or a service offense under the *National Defence Act* for which there was a fine of more than $5,000, a period of detention or imprisonment in excess of six months).

The PBC can deny a record suspension if it finds that an applicant is not of "good conduct." However, that person may reapply after one year.

The PBC may also revoke a record suspension for several reasons, including:

- A person is no longer of good conduct.

- A false or deceptive statement was made, or relevant information was concealed at the time of the application.

- The person is later convicted of a summary offense under a federal act or regulation.

- The records of the offenses would again be retained with the other conviction records.

If a person is subsequently convicted of an indictable offense under a federal act or regulation; an offense punishable either on indictable or summary conviction, or the PBC is convinced by new information that the person was ineligible for a record suspension at the time it was ordered, the suspension or pardon would cease to have effect and the record of the offenses would be retained.

> - **Number of record suspensions granted from 2012 to 2013: 612 with a grant rate of 82 percent.**
> - **Number of record suspensions ordered from 2012 to 2013: 6,030 with a grant rate of 97 percent.**

Note: Since 1970, more than 460,000 Canadians have received pardons and record suspensions; 96 percent of these are still in force, indicating that the vast majority of pardon-record suspension recipients remain crime-free in the community.[1]

1. Applying for a Record Suspension

The Parole Board of Canada (PBC) charges $631 to process a record-suspension application, with payment in the form of a certified check, bank draft, or money order payable to the Receiver General of Canada.

The applicant is also responsible for fees related to fingerprints, a copy of the individual's criminal record, court documents, and local police-record checks.

Applications seeking a record suspension for a summary offense will be processed within six months of application acceptance, while those involving an offense or offenses tried by indictment are processed within 12 months, according to the PBC. Applications in which the board is proposing to refuse to order a record suspension will require up to 24 months after application acceptance to complete.

There is no need to apply for a record suspension if a criminal record only consists of an absolute or a conditional discharge handed down by a court on or after July 24, 1992, since they are automatically removed from Canadian Police Information Centre (CPIC) one year (for an absolute discharge) or three years (for a conditional discharge) following the court decision.

To remove discharges given before July 24, 1992, from a record, the individual must contact the RCMP at the following address:

---

1 "PBC Facts," Parole Board of Canada, accessed March 2015. http://www.pbc-clcc.gc.ca/infocntr/factsh/parole_stats-eng.shtml

Royal Canadian Mounted Police
Record Suspension and Purge Services
PO Box 8885
Ottawa, ON K1G 3M8
Website: http://www.rcmp-grc.gc.ca/cr-cj/pp-er-eng.htm

The Request to Purge Absolute and/or Conditional Discharge can be found at http://www.rcmp-grc.gc.ca/form/3953-eng.pdf. (See Sample 4.)

Requests must contain the following information:

- Full name, including any maiden names or aliases.

- Date of birth.

- Return mailing address, including civic address, apartment number and/or PO box number, and postal code.

- Phone number including the area code.

- Details about the offense(s) that apply.

The RCMP's Record Suspension and Purge Services processes record suspensions, revocations, and the cessation of record suspensions; it also seals or reactivates the criminal record when a record suspension is granted, revoked, or ceases to have effect.

2. From Prisoner to Premier

The Wild West reputation from Yukon's Gold Rush days never quite left the territory, with its politicians facing convictions for perjury to breach of public trust over the past half-century.[2] But they committed their crimes while in office. Dennis Fentie did time for his before rising to Yukon's highest office.

Born in Edmonton on November 8, 1950, Fentie and his family moved to Watson Lake, a southeast Yukon town, in 1962. He worked at various jobs in logging, mining, and trucking, but in 1974, the future politician was convicted for heroin trafficking and sentenced to three years in a federal penitentiary. Fentie served 17 months in two prisons in Saskatchewan. Two decades later, he applied for and obtained a pardon, which sealed his criminal record.

---

2 "Yukon Politicians Far from Pure As Driven Snow," Paul Watson, *Toronto Star*, accessed February 2015. http://www.thestar.com/news/canada/2011/04/09/yukon_politicians_far_from_pure_as_driven_snow.html

Sample 4
Request to Purge Absolute and/or Conditional Discharge

Royal Canadian   Gendarmerie royale
Mounted Police   du Canada

Protected B
when completed

Request to Purge Absolute and / or Conditional Discharge

Please print legibly.

Requester Information
Name and Full Mailing Address of Requester

Discharge
I am hereby requesting the purge of my absolute discharge and / or conditional discharge from the central repository of the Royal Canadian Mounted Police.

Type of discharge	Date of Discharge - Approximate Date, if Actual Date Unknown (yyyy-mm-dd)
☐ Absolute ☐ Conditional	

Offences
Type of Offences Committed

Name Under Which the Sentence was Rendered

Date of Birth (yyyy-mm-dd)	Residence Telephone Number	Business Telephone Number

_____
Signature

_____
Date (yyyy-mm-dd)

Mail or send by facsimile to:

Legislative Conformity
Royal Canadian Mounted Police
Box 8885
Ottawa, Ontario
K1G 3M8

Facsimile: 613-957-9063

RCMP GRC 3953e (2013-04)   Page 1 of 1   Canadä

"I wanted my criminal record sealed so it would no longer be used against my character," says Fentie, who explains that he sought what has become known as a record suspension because he wanted to pursue politics.

That strategy worked. The same year (1996) he received his pardon, Fentie was elected a New Democratic Party (NDP) member of Yukon's Legislative Assembly for his home riding of Watson Lake. He left the NDP in May 2002 when he joined the Yukon Party, remained the MLA for Watson Lake, and was elected party leader a month later. Later that year when Yukoners went to the polls in November, the Yukon Party won 12 of the 18 seats available in the legislature to form a majority government — and Fentie became Yukon's seventh premier, serving in that role for two terms in two consecutive majority governments until his retirement from politics in 2011.

It was, as Fentie now recalls, "quite a trip" and offers what could be a punchy title should he ever write a memoir: "From the Penitentiary to the Premier's Office."

It should also be noted there was no Yukon legislation banning Fentie from seeking elected office. He opted for a pardon to "clean the slate." His criminal record was never an issue with Yukon voters. "In a small jurisdiction like the Yukon, most people knew about my past anyway," Fentie offers.

The issue only arose when he became Yukon Party leader and the *Yukon News* reported about it. (Crossing the border into the United States was never an issue either. As premier, Fentie had a US entry visa.)

However, he believes anyone with a criminal record should be given the opportunity for the fresh start a record suspension brings.

"I think it's important for an individual to be able to point to the fact that the justice system the Government of Canada have deemed you a changed and contributing person to society," says Fentie, who while retired is still active in Yukon's mining community as a member of the board of directors of Whitehorse-based Golden Predator Mining Corp. and as a consultant for Selwyn Chihong Mining Ltd., headquartered in Vancouver.

In 2014, he also helped a young Watson Lake resident — around the age Fentie was when he received his narcotics-related conviction — apply for a record suspension.

"He was refused initially, but I encouraged him to re-apply and he received the pardon," says Fentie. "He now has his own plumbing business in Red Deer, Alberta."

Fentie only had to apply once to receive his pardon, and he believes it was the result of good character references and the fact that he had "gone so long without being in trouble" between the time he was released from prison to the time he filed his application.

"There was a long period where all I did was work and pay taxes, so I had a good history. For others, who may have gotten into trouble subsequent to their serving a sentence, it might be a different story," says Fentie. "But for those who are worthy of it, our society provides a second chance."

3. Tough on Pardons

Following the revelation that two men convicted of sexual assault — former Toronto private-school teacher Clark Noble and former junior hockey coach Graham James — received pardons in 2006 and 2007 respectively prompted Prime Minister Stephen Harper's Conservative government to make it tougher to obtain a pardon.

In 2011, the Canadian government tabled Bill C-10, an omnibus crime bill entitled the *Safe Streets and Communities Act*, which was passed into law the following year and made various changes to Canada's criminal justice system, including the pardon process. For one thing, the word "pardon" was replaced with "record suspension." The ineligibility period to apply for a record suspension regarding an indictable offense was also increased from five to ten years, and for minor or summary conviction offenses from three to five years.

If you've been convicted of a sexual offense involving a minor, you can never apply for a record suspension — nor can you if you've been convicted of three or more indictable offenses.

The cost to obtain a record suspension also quadrupled from $150 to $631. (Before the federal Conservatives came to power in 2006, there was no charge to apply for a pardon.)

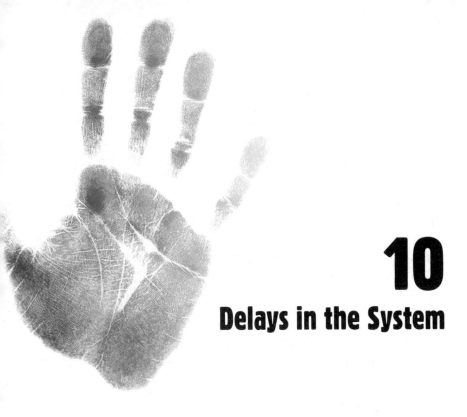

10

Delays in the System

Relying on statistics under Canada's access-to-information law, *The Canadian Press* (CP) reported in 2013, that between March 2012 and December 2012, there were 15,871 applications for criminal record suspensions, or a 40 percent decrease on an annualized basis from 2009 to 2010. Other stats showed that 3,693 record suspensions were granted from March 13, 2012, when the new rules under C-10 were enacted, compared to more than 24,000 granted in 2009 to 2010, the last full year before the federal government began changing the system, according to CP.[1]

The Parole Board of Canada (PBC) used to send back about 25 percent of applications for various reasons, CP reported. In 2012, the "error rate" was more than 45 percent.

The situation hasn't improved. In late 2014, CP reported that nearly 7,000 pardon applications were "in limbo" as the PBC is focusing its efforts on summary convictions rather than on pardon applications for more serious, indictable offenses.

1   "New Rules Make for Massive Drop in Pardons," *The Globe and Mail*, accessed March 2015. http://www.theglobeandmail.com/news/world/new-rules-make-for-massive-drop-in-pardons/article7217712/

The board told CP in March 2013 that it would clear a backlog of 22,000 older applications within two years, but said in November 2014 that it still has more than 10,000 applications remaining. In response to a media inquiry from CP, the PBC said the goal is to clear all files dealing with summary offenses ç and close to 70 percent of the overall number — by March 31, 2015, leaving 6,963 applications for indictable offenses in the backlog.

The PBC acknowledged the delay in a notice posted on its website for those who submitted pardon applications between July 2010 and February 22, 2012. "Applications for indictable offenses will be processed as resources permit following the completion of applications for summary offenses in the backlog." The board explained the delay is the result of June 2010 amendments to the *Criminal Records Act* that "significantly increased the complexity and amount of work required" to process a pardon application. "The user fee at that time [$50], which was already unsustainable, did not cover the additional costs needed to process a pardon under these amendments," resulting in the backlog.[2]

The PBC said it has taken "significant steps" to address the delay by reducing the backlog by more than 55 percent — from a total of 22,320 to just over 10,000 — and expects, as CP reported, to have nearly 70 percent of the remaining applications cleared by March 31, 2015.

Still, newer applications for record suspensions received on or after March 13, 2012, have a priority over pardon applications received on or after June 29, 2010, and before March 13, 2012, according to the PBC.

It explains that record suspensions operate under a full-cost recovery model ($631 user fee). Under the *User Fees Act*, these applications must by law be processed according to specific service standards:

- Up to 6 months for a summary offense.

- Up to 12 months for an indictable offense.

- Up to 24 months where the Board proposes to refuse.

Although pardon applicants may withdraw their application at any time and for any reason, they should first check that they

2 "Important Notice for Pardon Applicants in the Backlog," Parole Board of Canada, accessed March 2015. http://www.pbc-clcc.gc.ca/prdons/backlog-eng.shtml

qualify for a record suspension under the current *Criminal Records Act* **before** withdrawing their pardon application, as the eligibility requirements have changed, the PBC advises.

Since work to process pardon applications in the backlog has already been completed up to the investigation stage, no refund can be given for those who decide to withdraw their application.

Note: If applicants choose to withdraw their pardon application and re-apply for a record suspension, the board will transfer their pardon application to the record-suspension program. To withdraw a pardon application and re-apply for a record suspension, the PBC must receive the following:

- A signed letter from the applicants stating they wish to discontinue their pardon application; that they acknowledge that they will not be refunded the $150 pardon fee; and that they will submit an application for a record suspension.

- A completed and signed Record Suspension Application form (see Sample 5).

- A new completed Local Police Records Check (LPRC): All other documents remain valid and do *not* need to be resubmitted. (See Sample 6 for an example of a Local Police Records Check.)

- Payment of the $631 record suspension fee.

Applicants should consult the "Record Suspension Application Guide" (http://pbc-clcc.gc.ca/prdons/pardoninstr-eng.shtml) to learn more about record suspensions, including how to apply and pay for an application). Please note the download kit contains links to all the forms mentioned in this book.

1. Private Agencies

The rules have become so onerous that the odds are stacked against people with criminal records, explains Azmairnin Jadavji, President and Chief Executive Officer of Pardon Services Canada (PSC).

He explains that since the new rules came into effect in 2012, 20 percent of record suspension applications have been rejected and a three-member Parole Board panel, which meets on-camera and decides the merits of every application, sometimes denies

Sample 5
Record Suspension Application

Parole Board of Canada | Commission des libérations conditionnelles du Canada

Protected when completed

Record Suspension Application Form

Please print clearly using blue or black ink. You must answer all questions.

SECTION A: PERSONAL INFORMATION – You must answer all questions.

1. **What is your full legal name?** (You must fill in your name and date of birth at the top of page 2 as well.)

   Last Name: _____ Given Name(s): _____

2. **Have you ever used another name other than your legal name above?**

   NO ☐   YES ☐ → If YES, write these other names below or your application will be returned to you.

Previous Last Name(s)	Previous Given Name(s)

3. **What is your gender?** MALE ☐   FEMALE ☐   4. **What is your date of birth?** | Y | Y | Y | Y | M | M | D | D |

5. **Were you born in Canada?** NO ☐   YES ☐ → If NO, see STEP 5 of the Record Suspension Application Guide.

6. **Do you have a Driver's Licence?** NO ☐   YES ☐ → If YES, what is your Driver's Licence number?

   Number: _____ Province: _____

7. **Are you employed?** NO ☐   YES ☐ → If YES, who is your employer?

   Employer Name: _____

SECTION B: CORRESPONDENCE AND RESIDENCE INFORMATION – You must answer all questions.

8. **What is your Mailing Address?**

   (All information about a decision will be sent to your current address)

   _____

   Apartment/House Number and Street Address   City/Town   Province   Postal Code   Country

9. **Do you want information in English or French?** English ☐   French ☐

10. **What addresses have you lived at in the last 10 years?** Include your current address. **P.O. Boxes will not be accepted.**

Apartment/House Number and Street Address	City/Town	Province	Country	From Y Y Y Y M M	To Y Y Y Y M M
Current Address					Present
Previous Address					
Previous Address					
Previous Address					
Previous Address					

Please turn this form over. →

Parole Board of Canada   Toll-free Info line 1-800-874-2652 – www.recordsuspension.gc.ca   Canada

PBC/CLCC 0301E (2012)

I✦I Parole Board of Canada   Commission des libérations conditionnelles du Canada

Page 2 of 2

Protected when completed

Record Suspension Application Form

Please print clearly using blue or black ink. You must answer all questions.

APPLICANT INFORMATION – YOU MUST FILL IN THIS INFORMATION.

Indicate the full legal name and date of birth of the applicant provided on the front of this form:

Full legal name: _____ Date of birth: |Y|Y|Y|Y|M|M|D|D|

CONTACT INFORMATION – You must answer all questions. The Parole Board will need to contact you directly.

11. Telephone Number: (   )   -   → Can we leave a voicemail message? YES ☐ NO ☐

    If you do not have a telephone, provide a mailing address: _____

12. **Can we contact someone else about your application?**

    NO ☐ YES ☐ → If YES give us their name and telephone number:

    Name: _____ Telephone Number: (_____) _____-_____

13. **Have you ever been a member of the Canadian Forces?**

    ☐ NO   ☐ YES – Former   If **YES**, See Step 3 of the Record
                   ☐ YES – Current   Suspension Application Guide and
                   ☐ YES – Former or Current Reserve Member   fill in the information below.

    Military Service ID Number: _____

    Date of Enrolment: |Y|Y|Y|Y|M|M|D|D| Date of Discharge: |Y|Y|Y|Y|M|M|D|D|

    Provide the complete mailing address of your unit (your commanding officer may be contacted).

    Unit Name   Sub-Unit Name   Street Address or P.O. Box Number   City/Town   Province   Postal Code

CONVICTION INFORMATION – You must answer all questions.

14. **Do you have any other convictions that do not appear on your Criminal Record?**

    NO ☐ YES ☐ → If YES provide details below:

Offence	Arresting Police	Sentence	Date	Court (Street/City/Province)
Offence	Arresting Police	Sentence	Date	Court (Street/City/Province)
Offence	Arresting Police	Sentence	Date	Court (Street/City/Province)

APPLICANT AUTHORIZATION – You must answer all questions.

15. The information you provide in this application is collected under the authority of the *Criminal Records Act* for the purpose of processing your request for a record suspension. You have the right to the correction of, access to and protection of, your personal information under the *Privacy Act*. Personal information collected through the processing of your application will be stored in Personal Information Bank Number PBC PPU 010 and can be accessed and assessed for accuracy by sending a written request to the Access to Information and Privacy Coordinator, Parole Board of Canada, 410 Laurier Avenue West, Ottawa, ON K1A 0R1. Exempt personal information obtained from external partners in the course of processing this application cannot be provided upon request.

You must sign and date this form to confirm the following: I understand that the information may be used in a record suspension decision, to conduct inquiries, and may be used in summary form for reporting, quality control, performance measurement, evaluation, research purposes and to establish an inventory of record suspensions. I grant permission for the disclosure of relevant personal information about me with justice system participants as defined in the *Criminal Code*, as may be deemed necessary for the purpose of the investigation related to this application and for the purpose of any record suspension decision.

I certify that the statements made by me in this application are true and complete. Failure to sign this authorization will result in your application being returned to you as incomplete.

Sign here: _____ Date: |Y|Y|Y|Y|M|M|D|D|

(Applicant's Signature)

PBC/CLCC 0301E (2012)

Sample 6
Local Police Records Check

I✦I Parole Board of Canada / Commission des libérations conditionnelles du Canada

Page 1 of 2

Protected when completed

Local Police Records Check Form
For the purpose of a Record Suspension Application
Please print clearly using blue or black ink. You must answer all questions.

SECTION A: PERSONAL INFORMATION – You must answer all questions.

1. **What is your full legal name?** (You must fill in your name and date of birth at the top of page 2 as well.)

   Last Name: _____ Given Name(s): _____

2. **Have you ever used another name other than your legal name above?**
   NO ☐   YES ☐ → If YES, write these other names below or your application will be returned to you.

Previous Last Name(s)	Previous Given Name(s)

3. **What is your gender?** MALE ☐ FEMALE ☐   4. **What is your date of birth?** Y Y Y Y M M D D

5. **Do you have a Driver's Licence?** NO ☐ YES ☐ → If YES, what is your Driver's Licence number?
   Number: _____ Province: _____

SECTION B: MAILING AND RESIDENCE INFORMATION – You must answer all questions.

6. **What is your mailing address?**

   _____

   Apartment/House Number and Street Address　　City/Town　　Province　　Postal Code　　Country

7. **What is your telephone number?** (_____) ____ - _____

8. **What addresses have you lived at in the last 5 years?** Include your current address. P.O. Boxes will not be accepted.

Apartment/House Number and Street Address	City/Town	Province	Country	From Y Y Y Y M M	To Y Y Y Y M M
Current Address					Present
Previous Address					
Previous Address					
Previous Address					

SECTION C: APPLICANT AUTHORIZATION – You must sign and date here.

9. **You must write in the name of the Police Service, and then <u>you</u> must sign and date this form.**
   I hereby authorize (write in name of Police Service here) _____
   to release to the Parole Board of Canada information that the Police is allowed to divulge.
   Sign here: _____ Date: Y Y Y Y M M D D
   　　　　(Applicant's Signature)

10. **Ask the Police Service to fill in the <u>back</u> of this form.** Include this form in your application with the front side filled in **by you** and the back side filled in by the **Police Service.**

Please turn this form over. →

Parole Board of Canada ▪ Toll-free Info line 1-800-874-2652 – www.recordsuspension.gc.ca Canadä

PBC/CLCC 0301E (2012)

Sample 6 — Continued

Parole Board of Canada / Commission des libérations conditionnelles du Canada

Page 2 of 2

Protected when completed

Local Police Records Check Form

For the purpose of a Record Suspension Application
Please print clearly using blue or black ink. You must answer all questions.

SECTION D: FOR POLICE USE ONLY. DO NOT WRITE IN THIS SECTION.

Indicate the full legal name and date of birth of the applicant provided on the front of this form:

Full legal name: _____ Date of birth: `Y Y Y Y M M D D`

Are There Convictions in Addition to Those Appearing on CPIC? ☐ NO ☐ YES

Conviction(s) in Addition to Those Appearing on CPIC

Offence Description	Sentence	Place of Sentence	Arresting Police Service	Date of Sentence Y Y Y Y M M D D

List all Information Related to Incidents Involving Police and All Charges Regardless of Disposition Including Provincial Convictions/Charges.

Nature of Occurrence	Outcome	File Number	Date of Occurrence Y Y Y Y M M D D

Police Representative Information:

Police Service Name: _____

Police Representative Name: _____ Telephone Number: (_____) _____ - _____

Signature: _____

Date: `Y Y Y Y M M D D` | Internal Use Only |

Please put Police Service seal or stamp here

PBC/CLCC 0301E (2012)

them for "very frivolous reasons." Says Jadavji: "If an application regarding an impaired driving charge goes before the tribunal, it could be denied just because the person was also speeding."

He explains that he decided to drop out of law school and establish PSC in 1989 — the first agency of its kind in Canada at the time — when he realized that 13 percent of the Canadian population had a criminal record and most were unaware they could apply for what was then a pardon.

Demand was so high for PSC's services that pardon applications to the Parole Board jumped from 800 to more than 2,000 a month in its first year of operation, according to Jadavji.

"We created an industry and now have about 45 competitors in Canada. But most of those companies are one-man shops, which is a problem if someone gets sick, goes on holiday, or gets hit by a truck."

He says that PSC employs 18 people at its Vancouver headquarters as well as satellite offices in Edmonton, Calgary, Toronto, Ottawa, and Montreal, which complete and file applications on behalf of clients in what can become a complicated process.

For instance, courts and police services have different rules — and fees — regarding accessing criminal record documentation. PSC handles that, says Jadavji, and can resubmit an application that was denied following a one-year waiting period while he notes that time is of the essence.

"Let's say someone convicted of a summary offense for smoking a joint is in a four-year program to become a nurse. That person has to wait five years before even applying for a record suspension, which will further delay finding a job."

Sometimes, as he points out, people get saddled with a criminal record for a minor offense without having committed it. "When I had just started my business, I had a client who contacted me and wanted some literature sent to him at a post office box under an alias. He was embarrassed about his record and made an appointment at a time there would be no other clients in the office."

"What happened was he walked out of a Safeway with shopping bags and a security guard asked to see a receipt. He said his wife had it, but the security guy didn't believe him, and he was charged with shoplifting. He didn't even do anything, but he was a newcomer to the country and pled guilty and received a summary conviction." Jadavji got the man a pardon.

However, for the estimated 50 percent of Canadians who file their own applications, it may not be as easy, he says, noting that 45 percent of those who submit their own record-suspension applications are rejected. "If it weren't for advocates like us vigorously arguing individual cases before the Parole Board, some folks wouldn't have a chance."

For clients, PSC assists with or obtains the following (pardon-servicescanada.com):

- Canadian Police Information Centre (CPIC) criminal record check ($25).

- Fingerprinting, which is required to obtain a certified criminal record, for a fee ranging from $25 to $80 — depending on the police service — along with a $35 administration fee.

- All court documents confirming the sentence has been served (administration fee $20 or court fee, whichever is higher).

- Criminal record check from the local police detachment in each municipality the client lived in over the last five years (administration fee is the greater of $60 or the current police department levy — and some police departments require the client to attend).

- Conduct report for past or present members of the Canadian Armed Forces ($25 administration fee).

- Documentation demonstrating reformation of character and verification of the victim's age regarding sexual-offense convictions.

- Declaration as to how a record suspension would provide a "measurable benefit and sustain rehabilitation into society as a law-abiding citizen."

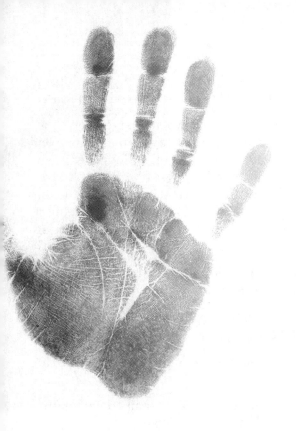

11
Your Rights

The *Canadian Human Rights Act* forbids discrimination based on a record suspended conviction, which includes services a person needs or the opportunity to work for a federal agency.

The *Criminal Records Act* states that no employment application form within the federal public service may ask any question that would require an applicant to disclose a conviction. This also applies to a Crown corporation, the Canadian Armed Forces, or any business within the federal authority.

However, a record suspension will not cancel prohibition orders, regarding driving or firearms possession, imposed under the *Criminal Code*.

Anyone convicted of an offense as an adult under a federal act or regulation in Canada may apply for a record suspension, whether that person is a Canadian citizen or a resident of Canada. A person may also apply if he or she was convicted in another country and was transferred to Canada under the *Transfer of Offenders Act*. However, anyone convicted of a sexual offense involving a child (under Schedule 1 of the *Criminal Records Act*) or has more than three offenses prosecuted by indictment each with a prison sentence of two years or more is ineligible for a record suspension.

A record suspension is not required when charges were dismissed, stayed, or withdrawn, and did not result in a conviction. However, if the record is on the RCMP system, an individual may contact the arresting police force and request that the RCMP return the fingerprints and all of the information obtained at the time of the arrest for destruction. The RCMP can deny a request to destroy a non-conviction record if one or more of the following conditions apply:

- The applicant was not an adult relative to the charge as defined within the *Youth Criminal Justice Act*.

- The applicant has a criminal conviction on file within the RCMP's National Repository of Criminal Records.

- The applicant has an outstanding criminal charge before the courts.

- The appeal period has not expired for a non-conviction record relating to an acquittal or a dismissal.

- One year has not elapsed for a non-conviction record relating to either a peace bond or a stay of proceedings.

In addition to these conditions, a non-conviction record will be retained for a minimum of five years from the date of the court decision if the charge is related to the following:

- High treason or treason.

- Potential terrorist activity.

- First- and second-degree murder.

- Manslaughter.

- Aggravated assault.

- Sexual offenses.

The non-conviction record will also be retained for a minimum of five years when an individual is found not criminally responsible due to a mental disorder.

According to the RCMP, non-conviction information may be used by police agencies for operational activities, including crime-scene investigations, the identification of deceased persons, and those with amnesia. This information is "not normally" used for background checks or employment-screening purposes.

The RCMP has the legal right to keep this information under the Identification of *Criminals Act* and will retain it in the National Repository of Criminal Records until the police agency that laid the charge requests the information be destroyed — and the RCMP approves it. If approved, the RCMP will notify the police agency that made the request. If not, the RCMP will provide an explanation.

Requests to have records destroyed within the five-year period should be supported by additional information, such as Crown proceedings, police services records, and/or court documents.

The RCMP has introduced a new policy for the retention and destruction of non-conviction information that outlines the criteria the RCMP uses to determine whether non-conviction information contained in the National Repository of Criminal Records is retained or destroyed. "Non-conviction information" refers to criminal charges with court decisions other than "guilty," which include acquittals, withdrawals, stays of proceedings, peace bonds, and findings of "not guilty."

Criminal records are retained until the subject of the record reaches the age of 80 with no criminal activity reported in the previous ten years, except in the following circumstances:

- The person has been sentenced to life imprisonment.

- The person has been designated a "dangerous offender" and/or is still under a court sentence.

- The person is still under an unexpired prohibition order.

- The person has an outstanding warrant or an interest has been expressed by an agency engaged in the execution or administration of the law.

In each of those instances, the criminal record is held until the subject completes his or her sentence and has a clear criminal record for a ten-year period, and the subject has reached the age of 100.

Note that the policy only applies to non-conviction records stored in the National Repository of Criminal Records. (Local police agencies have their own policies regarding the management of non-conviction records that fall under their jurisdiction.)

An individual can appeal an RCMP decision to deny a request to destroy non-conviction information, but must identify an error in fact or process regarding the decision and/or cite new information not included in the original request along with supporting documentation, such as copies of applicable Crown proceedings, police-services records, and/or court documents.

To appeal a decision, contact:

Royal Canadian Mounted Police
ATTN: Director General
Canadian Criminal Real Time Identification Services
1200 Vanier Parkway, NPS Building
Ottawa, ON K1A 0R2
Phone: 613-998-6362

1. Fraud Alert

The Parole Board of Canada (PBC) is warning pardon applicants about some companies using symbols and visuals on their websites and marketing materials similar to the Canadian government's and/or making misleading claims and guarantees. As a result, the board reiterates that it's the only federal agency authorized to order a record suspension and that it can be identified by its official Government of Canada signature bloc (http://pbc-clcc.gc.ca/prdons/fraud-eng.shtml). The same site shows symbols and markings that have no affiliation with the PBC.

The board also reminds applicants that third-party companies can only prepare an application, and are neither involved in the decision-making process nor can influence it. Applicants should also ignore third-party claims that the record-suspension program is ending and to apply through them "before it's too late." As well, the PBC doesn't endorse any third-party companies that prepare record-suspension applications — and before using the services of one, the board recommends that you check them with your local Better Business Bureau (http://www.bbb.org/). The PBC's official website is www.pbc-clcc.gc.ca and can also be accessed at www.recordsuspension.gc.ca. You can also contact the PBC at 1-800-874-2652 or suspension@pbc-clcc.gc.ca.

Other websites that use "Parole Board of Canada" in their name or domain name or use Canadian government symbols are fraudulent — such as www.paroleboardofcanada.com or www.pardonscriminalrecords.ca — and should be reported to the Canadian Anti-Fraud Centre (CAFC) at its toll-free number (1-888-495-8501) or via email at info@antifraudcentre.ca. (Keep in mind that the CAFC isn't very responsive and you may not receive a reply or update on any complaint you file with the Centre.)

12
Young Offenders

If a young person is found guilty of a summary offense, the record is removed three years after the sentence is served, including custody and/or probation. If a conviction is entered on an indictable offense, the record remains active for five years after the sentence is satisfied (also including custody and/or probation) and is then transferred to a special repository.

If, prior to the expiration of the periods, a young person is subsequently found guilty of either a summary or indictable offense, the retention period for all entries begins again.

1. Extrajudicial Sanctions

Should a young person be acquitted — other than by a verdict of not criminally responsible on account of mental disorder — and the charge is dismissed, withdrawn, or stayed, the record is transferred to a special repository. If a youth receives a reprimand, extrajudicial sanctions, or is ordered to enter into a recognizance to keep the peace and maintain good behavior, the information is also transferred to a special repository.

According to the Canadian Federal Department of Justice, extrajudicial sanctions — such as volunteer work, victim compensation, and attending specialized programs imposed either before or after a young person is charged with an offense — are to be used only if other forms of extrajudicial measures, which are used as an alternative to laying charges would not be sufficient to hold a young person accountable.

2. Extrajudicial Measures

"Extrajudicial" means "outside the court" — thus extrajudicial measures aim to hold a young person accountable without proceeding through the formal court process, according to the Federal Justice Department.

Some examples of extrajudicial measures include:

- A police officer deciding that no further response to an incident is required.

- The police issue either a warning or a caution — a more formal warning that may, in some cases, require the young person and his or her parents to appear at the police station to discuss the incident.

Information regarding restorative justice or extrajudicial measures is destroyed upon receipt. If a young person is found guilty and given an absolute discharge, the record is transferred to a special repository one year from the sentencing date. If a youth is found guilty and handed a conditional discharge, the entry is transferred to a special repository three years from the date of sentence.

3. Disposition or Destruction of Records and Prohibition on Use and Disclosure

As the RCMP points out, law-enforcement agencies cannot access young-person information once it is removed to a special repository. Record Suspension and Purge Services can only release information stored there under circumstances outlined in section 128 of the *Youth Criminal Justice Act*.

Section 128.

(1) Subject to sections 123, 124, and 126, after the end of the applicable period set out in section 119 or 120 no record kept under sections 114 to 116 may be used for any purpose that would identify the young person to whom the record relates as a young person dealt with under this Act or the Young Offenders Act *chapter Y-1 of the Revised Statutes of Canada, 1985.*

...

Disposal of RCMP records

(3) All records kept under subsection 115(3) shall be destroyed or, if the Librarian and Archivist of Canada requires it, transmitted to the Librarian and Archivist, at the end of the applicable period set out in section 119 or 120.

Purging Canadian Police Information Centre (CPIC)

(4) The Commissioner of the Royal Canadian Mounted Police shall remove a record from the automated criminal conviction records retrieval system maintained by the Royal Canadian Mounted Police at the end of the applicable period referred to in section 119; however, information relating to a prohibition order made under an Act of Parliament or the legislature of a province shall be removed only at the end of the period for which the order is in force.

Exception

(5) Despite subsections (1), (2), and (4), an entry that is contained in a system maintained by the Royal Canadian Mounted Police to match crime-scene information and that relates to an offense committed or alleged to have been committed by a young person shall be dealt with in the same manner as information that relates to an offense committed by an adult for which a record suspension ordered under the Criminal Records Act *is in effect.*

...

Definition of "destroy"

(7) For the purposes of subsections (2) and (3), "destroy," in re-
spect of a record, means:

(a) to shred, burn, or otherwise physically destroy the record,
in the case of a record other than a record in electronic
form; and

(b) to delete, write over, or otherwise render the record inac-
cessible, in the case of a record in electronic form.

4. How to Apply

The "Record Suspension Application Guide" includes step-by-step
instructions on how to apply and includes the forms required (note
that the download kit includes link to the guide and forms). It also
outlines how to obtain required documents, such as the criminal
record; local police records checks; and other relevant information.

A completed record suspension application must include the
following:

- An original criminal record or certification of no criminal
record and proof of conviction documents, as required.

- Court information.

- A military conduct sheet (if applicable).

- Local police records check(s).

- Proof of citizenship or immigrants documents, if born outside Canada.

- A photocopy of a document to support your identity, such as
a driver's license or a health card.

You can find the "Record Suspension Application Guide" and
Forms online at: http://www.pbc-clcc.gc.ca/prdons/pardon-eng.
shtml

To locate RCMP detachments, go to: http://www.rcmp-grc.
gc.ca/detach/index-eng.htm.

You contact the Parole Board of Canada's national and regional
offices at the following:

Website: http://pbc-clcc.gc.ca/contus/offices-eng.shtml
Toll-free information line: 1-800-874-2652
Fax: 613-941-4981
Email: suspension@pbc-clcc.gc.ca

Or regular mail at:

Parole Board of Canada
410 Laurier Avenue West
Ottawa, ON K1A 0R1

The PBC must also be notified in writing of any address change while an application is being processed.

You do not require a lawyer or a representative to apply for a record suspension. According to the PBC, all record suspension applications are given equal consideration, regardless as to whether they are submitted by an individual or by a representative from a private agency. Hiring a lawyer or an agency "will not improve your chances of receiving a record suspension," and claims that suggest otherwise are "false and misleading," says the Board.

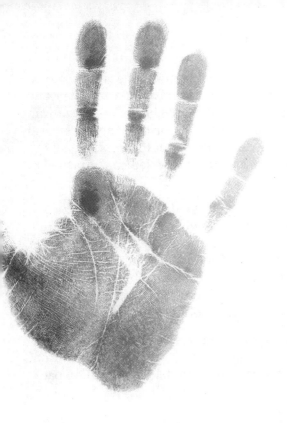

13

Entry Permits

Pardon Services Canada (PSC) helps clients obtain entry waivers for both the United States and Canada, and points out that anyone attempting to enter the US with a criminal record can be arrested and detained, deported, and have their property or vehicle confiscated. On the latter, Azmairnin Jadavji (President and Chief Executive Officer of PSC) notes that during the summer of 2014 alone, more than 5,000 vehicles owned by Canadians with criminal records were confiscated at the Washington-British Columbia border.

US Customs and Border Protection does not recognize Canadian record suspensions because it has access to criminal records of every Canadian dating back to the 1960s and relies on its own National Crime Information Center database, according to Andrew Maloney on the website USEntryWaiverLaw.ca, an immigration lawyer certified by the Law Society of Upper Canada as a foreign legal consultant who specializes in US immigration.

An entry waiver — a document issued by the US Department of Homeland Security under the *Immigration and Nationality Act* — is issued for one, two, or five years depending on several factors, such as the strength of the application, the seriousness and extent of the crimes committed, the amount of time since the convictions occurred, and whether or not it involves a new waiver or a renewal, explains USEntryWaiverLaw.ca. It says that a person can visit the US multiple times during the duration of a single US travel waiver, but if a stay is planned for more than three months, additional forms may need to be completed, notarized, and attached to the application known as a Form I-192.

Depending on the reason for your inadmissibility into the US, and if you are a class of nonimmigrant where a visa is not required, such as most citizens of Canada, you may be eligible to apply in advance of your travel directly to US Customs and Border Protection (CBP) for a temporary waiver of inadmissibility. The waiver application process can be lengthy (up to a year) and there is a cost of US $585 per application regardless of the decision.

The temporary waiver application, Form I-192, can be downloaded from the US CBP website (www.cbp.gov/travel/international-visitors/admission-forms). The Form I-192 application package must include the following:

- Evidence of citizenship.

- Completed and signed Form I-192.

- Properly executed Form G-28 (Notice of Entry of Appearance as Attorney of Accredited Representative) must be included with the application if an authorized person has been retained to represent the applicant.

- US fingerprint card (FD-258) to be completed by a US Customs and Border Protection officer when the application is submitted.

- Completed and signed Biographic Information Form (G-325A).

- Canadians must obtain verification of their criminal record, or evidence of a lack thereof, from the RCMP by submitting their fingerprints on Form C-216C available from a local police station or private accredited fingerprinting agency, which must be dated and endorsed by the RCMP within 15 months of submitting Form I-192.

- Copy of the official court record from the actual court of conviction indicating plea indictment, conviction, and disposition for each and every crime committed anywhere in the world.

- If you are inadmissible to the US because of a criminal conviction, you should submit a statement in your own words, signed by you, explaining the circumstances of each arrest, conviction, and sentence or fine imposed. In addition, you should submit any evidence or explanation of your reformation of character or rehabilitation such as counseling or rehabilitation programs completed, current employment, marital status, community service, or any other information you wish to be considered and that you believe strengthens your request.

- If you are inadmissible for health-related reasons, such as drug use or addiction, you will need to provide evidence of treatment and rehabilitation, including a recent drug test; credible, verifiable evidence related to rehabilitative history; statement from you making clear a commitment to refrain from using controlled substances in the US; credible, verifiable evidence outlining a program for substitution therapy/treatment, and/ or continued care relative to drug use/addiction if allowed to enter the US.

- If you've been previously been denied entry or removed from the US, you will also have to complete Form I-212 (Application for Permission to Reapply for Admission into the United States after Deportation or Removal).

Form I-192 and accompanying documents are filed in advance of travel at a major port of entry at the US border or a US Customs and Border Protection preclearance office in Canada.

According to US Customs and Border Protection, common reasons for inadmissibility include:

- Criminal record of multiple convictions.

- Criminal record for crimes of moral turpitude, such as murder, manslaughter, rape, theft, bribery, forgery, aggravated battery, prostitution, and fraud.

- Violation of any law or regulation related to a controlled substance, including but not limited to trafficking in a controlled substance.

- Involvement in human trafficking or money laundering.

- Have a communicable disease.

- Found to be a drug abuser or addict.

- Have overstayed a previous period of admission to the US.

This list is far from exhaustive. Moral turpitude also includes abandonment of a child, arson, assault, blackmail, bigamy, contributing to the delinquency of a minor, counterfeiting, extortion, incest, perjury, and willful tax evasion. If it's any consolation, crimes not involving moral turpitude include breaking and entering, disorderly conduct, drunkenness, gambling and liquor violations, juvenile delinquency, trespassing, and vagrancy.

However, if you've committed a crime of moral turpitude and it qualifies as a "petty offense" under the US *Immigration and Nationality Act*, you may still be able to enter the US without a waiver. A petty offense is one in which the maximum penalty is one year or less, and the person was sentenced to no more than six months imprisonment (the exact amount of time the person actually spent in jail doesn't matter).

1. Other Reasons for Inadmissibility to the USA

The following sections includes a comprehensive list detailing other reasons for inadmissibility to the US.

1.1 Health reasons

Health reasons include communicable diseases, such as gonorrhea, leprosy, syphilis, venereum, lymphogranuloma, inguinale, granuloma, chancroid, class-A tuberculosis, as well as select physical and mental disorders as determined by the US Secretary of Health and Human Services.

An individual who refuses the required vaccinations to enter the country may be refused entry as well. A person who is diagnosed with one of the above illnesses can apply for a US entry waiver using form I-601, although there are several additional application requirements that will need to be met depending on the disease.

1.2 Security

Anyone accused of or convicted of being a saboteur, terrorist, or a spy requires a travel waiver. Persons who are voluntary members of the communist party or any other type of totalitarian party, including Nazis, and any persons who would be an endangerment to US foreign policy will also need special permission to enter the US, which requires they prove that they are not a threat to the general public of the country.

1.3 Immigration violators and illegal entrants

A person who has entered the US without being paroled or admitted at a valid port of entry, or a person who overstays his or her time in the country will accrue an unlawful presence.

The time frame for the ban will depend on how long the person was in the country illegally. A person who is found to be inadmissible because he or she has been unlawfully present in the country for more than 180 days will receive a three-year ban and those who enter and stay for more than a year will receive a ten-year ban.

Anyone who has left the US voluntarily can apply for a waiver based on overstay inadmissibility using form I-601, which also applies to anyone who has knowingly or willfully committed fraud or made misrepresentations to obtain some type of immigration benefit. A person who has been deported or been given expedited removal will also need to file another form, I-212, which is an application to reapply for admission provided he or she is seeking nonimmigrant entry.

Any person who has been in the US unlawfully for more than a year and has exited the country and then re-entered without being inspected will also need to file a US entry waiver form to have his or her unlawful presence waived.

1.4 Falsely claiming US citizenship

An alien who has falsely claimed US citizenship after Sept. 30, 1996, will not be eligible for any type of US waiver under the *Immigration and Nationality Act* and will be banned from entering the country for life, except in extreme circumstances.

1.5 Military service

Anyone who left the US to avoid conscription or a person who unlawfully left the US Armed Forces and has not regularized his or her status in the US may have an outstanding warrant for their arrest or may be ineligible to enter the country. Anyone unsure about this can contact the nearest Customs and Border Protection or Department of Homeland Security office and inquire about their status.

Even those individuals who were not in the military, but left the US on uncertain terms, may find there is a warrant for their arrest in the US. If this is the case, and you attempt to enter the country, you will be arrested on your arrival and sent to the state from where the warrant against you was issued.

1.6 Miscellaneous grounds for inadmissibility

Miscellaneous grounds for inadmissibility include the following:

- Being a practising polygamist.

- A guardian who is accompanying a helpless alien.

- International child abductors and family members who support abductors.

- Former US citizens found by the Attorney General to have renounced their citizenship as a way to avoid paying taxes owed to the Internal Revenue Service.

US waivers may be granted for several humanitarian purposes, such as allowing a family to stay together or in cases of extreme hardship. This applies when the applicant is the spouse, parent, daughter, son, brother, sister, or fiancé(e) of a US citizen; or is the son, daughter, or spouse of a lawful permanent resident of the US.

However, if at first you don't succeed at attempting to cross the Canada-US border, do *not* try again, USEntryWaiverLaw.ca strongly advises. "If you have already been denied entry to the US, it's extremely important that you abide by the instructions and do not attempt to return until you are legally allowed to do so. At this point it is pointless to argue with US Customs and Border Protection about its decision to refuse you entry, and you should instead focus on how you can get pre-approved for re-entry by contacting a US immigration attorney. If you attempt to re-enter the US at another port of entry after previously being turned away, not only will you be denied entrance once again but you also risk being banned from the country for an extensive amount of time."

The website also addresses circumstances in which a person, who obtained either a conditional or absolute discharge after being convicted of a crime, may also be deemed inadmissible to the US since the discharge is still considered evidence of guilt. "For this reason the same rules apply to a discharge as to a conviction, meaning a conditional discharge or absolute discharge for a given crime will be treated by US border agents in a similar manner to a conviction for that crime."

Absolute discharges remain on a person's record for a year while conditional discharges stay on a person's record for three years. If you've received such a discharge, you should obtain a criminal record check after the one- or three-year time period is completed to make sure that it has been completely removed. Should it not be removed from your record, the courts may have recorded the discharge as a conviction and it won't be automatically purged after it expires. Or, the discharge could be removed from the RCMP database successfully but a FingerPrints Section (FPS) number still associated with your name might not have been properly purged as well which could still lead to a positive hit at the Canada-US border.

2. What a Lawyer Can Do for You

If you plan on entering the US with a criminal discharge, bring along a legal opinion letter — prepared by a lawyer — that will explain your situation to US immigration authorities.

A lawyer can do much more, beginning with ensuring the US entry waiver application is complete, accurate, and error-free. A law firm can assist you with any additional documentation you may need to help your application. Lawyers can also help you prepare for your interview and coach you on how to best explain your situation to border officials.

Even with the US $585 application fee, the US Department of Homeland Security only accepts cheques and money orders drawn from American financial institutions, which is a major problem for the vast majority of Canadians who do not have a US bank account. However, you can pay the fee, using a credit card or other form of payment, to a lawyer who will forward it the US government.

If an individual already has a nonimmigrant visa, such as the popular H-1B that allows American companies to employ Canadians in specialty occupations, a US Waiver is still needed to overcome criminal inadmissibility (including for alien re-entry).

Note that a US entry waiver also allows you to travel over US airspace, which is otherwise prohibited if you have a criminal record.

3. Getting into Canada

Pardon Services Canada (PSC) helps visitors with criminal records, including those involving minor offenses, such as driving under the influence — who might otherwise be denied entry to Canada — obtain temporary resident permits (TRPs) from Citizenship and Immigration Canada, or "criminal rehabilitation" status and be allowed into the country. An individual is considered inadmissible if the equivalent crime carries a prison term exceeding ten years.

According to PSC, such a person is deemed "rehabilitated" after ten years since completion of the sentence, although that individual can apply for a TRP if five years have passed.

PSC has prepared some tips for Americans with a criminal record attempting to enter Canada with a TRP.

- Know the details of your conviction. Even if you weren't convicted, the arrest or charge might still appear when a search is conducted.

- Don't assume a "minor" conviction will not be an issue when trying to cross the border into Canada. A misdemeanor in the US, such as a DUI/DWI may be considered a more serious offense in Canada.

- Demonstrate the need to enter Canada offsets any health or safety risks to Canada.

- Submit a copy of the travel itinerary and/or airline ticket and any other travel documentation as part of the application.

- Plan ahead since processing times can range from 30 to 45 days.

- Don't lie because that can result in never being allowed entry to Canada.

Online applications are not accepted, and the application fee for a TRP is $200 CND and is nonrefundable regardless of whether or not the permit is granted. More information can be found online at http://www.cic.gc.ca/english/information/inadmissibility/permits.asp.

PSC's fees range from $595, for basic service with a "guaranteed" accepted application of 18 months, to $1,950 for expedited service, in which it guarantees an application will be accepted within 10 months. You can find the agency on the web at PardonServicesCanada.com.

14
Royal Prerogative of Mercy

According to the Parole Board of Canada (PBC), the royal prerogative of mercy was vested in the British sovereign under common
law and arose as a way to compensate for the law's "inequities and
imperfections," one of which was that before 1836, a person on
trial for a capital crime in what is now Canada had no right to legal
counsel. Furthermore, it wasn't until 1898 that someone accused
of a capital crime, which carried the death penalty, was allowed to
testify in court on his or her own behalf. A condemned person was
not allowed to appeal a death sentence until 1907.

Appeals for clemency, or mercy, from a convicted person's family, friends, employer, or parish priest or, as the PBC notes, sometimes even the judge who imposed the sentence, would be sent to
the colonial governor who could use the royal prerogative to commute a sentence of capital punishment sentence imposed for those
convicted of murder, rape, or treason.

In 1976, the death penalty in Canada was abolished — the
same year the royal prerogative of mercy was transferred to the
PBC, which makes recommendations for the exercise of clemency

either by the Governor General or the Governor in Council (the federal Cabinet).

Historically, according to the PBC, clemency was granted to the following:

- The extremely young or old.
- Those with low intelligence.
- The insane.
- When a crime was not premeditated or when drunkenness was involved when the crime was committed.
- Due to a recommendation for mercy from the trial judge or jury.
- In light of "community sentiment" such as in the case of a woman who was the mother of eight children.

Clemency is granted in exceptional circumstances in deserving cases involving federal offenses where no other remedy exists in law to reduce severe negative effects of criminal sanctions. It can be requested for several reasons, including employment, perceived inequity, medical conditions, immigration to Canada, compassion, and financial hardship.

The Governor General or the Governor in Council grants clemency upon the recommendation of a Minister of the Crown — most often the Minister of Public Safety. However, as the PBC points out, if you're ineligible for a record suspension or the board has refused to order a record suspension in your case, it's "highly unlikely" you will qualify for a royal prerogative of mercy.

> **Number of royal prerogatives of mercy granted in 2012: 52 requests received, 12 granted.[1]**

1. Types of Clemency

Under sections 748 and 748.1 of Canada's *Criminal Code*, the Governor in Council can grant the following types of clemency:

---

1 "PBC Facts," Parole Board of Canada, accessed March 2015.
http://www.pbc-clcc.gc.ca/infocntr/factsh/parole_stats-eng.shtml

- A free pardon: Based on innocence, it is a recognition that the conviction was in error and erases the consequences and records of the conviction.

- A remission of fine, forfeiture, and pecuniary penalty: Erases all, or part of the monetary penalty that was imposed.

- A conditional pardon: The criminal record is kept separate and apart from other criminal records prior to pardon eligibility under the *Criminal Records Act* (five years for a summary offense, ten years for an indictable offense); or parole in advance of eligibility date under the *Corrections and Conditional Release Act* for offenders serving life and indeterminate sentences who are ineligible for parole by exception.

The following is section 748 of the *Criminal Code's* pardons and remissions information:

To whom pardon may be granted:

748.

(1) Her Majesty may extend the royal mercy to a person who is sentenced to imprisonment under the authority of an Act of Parliament, even if the person is imprisoned for failure to pay money to another person.

Free or conditional pardon

(2) The Governor in Council may grant a free pardon or a conditional pardon to any person who has been convicted of an offense.

Effect of free pardon

(3) Where the Governor in Council grants a free pardon to a person, that person shall be deemed thereafter never to have committed the offense in respect of which the pardon is granted.

Punishment for subsequent offense not affected

(4) No free pardon or conditional pardon prevents or mitigates the punishment to which the person might otherwise be lawfully sentenced on a subsequent conviction for an offense other than that for which the pardon was granted.

The Governor General can also grant free and conditional pardons, and the remission of fine, forfeiture, and pecuniary penalty. However, the Governor General's authority to grant clemency is normally only used when it is not possible to proceed under the *Criminal Code*.

However, there are certain types of clemency that can only be granted by the Governor General:

- Remission of sentence in which all or part of the sentence is erased.

- Respite or an interruption in the execution of the sentence.

- Relief from prohibition, in which there is alteration or removal of a prohibition, such as one from driving or possessing firearms.

The PBC may — under section 109 of the *Corrections and Conditional Release Act* on written application, cancel or vary the unexpired portion of a prohibition order made under section 259 of the *Criminal Code* after a period of either:

- Ten years after the commencement of the order, in the case of a prohibition for life.

- Five years after the commencement of the order, in the case of a prohibition for more than five years but less than life.

The Governor General may also grant relief from the prohibition if the time period required above has not been completed.

Here is section 259, mandatory order of prohibition:

(1) When an offender is convicted of an offense committed under section 253 or 254 or this section or discharged under section 730 of an offense committed under section 253 and, at the time the offense was committed or, in the case of an offense committed under section 254, within the three hours preceding that time, was operating or had the care or control of a motor vehicle, vessel or aircraft or of railway equipment or was assisting in the operation of an aircraft or of railway equipment, the court that sentences the offender shall, in addition to any other punishment that may be imposed for that offense, make an order prohibiting the offender from operating a motor vehicle on any street, road, highway, or

other public place, or from operating a vessel or an aircraft or railway equipment, as the case may be:

(a) *For a first offense, during a period of not more than three years plus any period to which the offender is sentenced to imprisonment, and not less than one year.*

(b) *For a second offense, during a period of not more than five years plus any period to which the offender is sentenced to imprisonment, and not less than two years.*

(c) *For each subsequent offense, during a period of not less than three years plus any period to which the offender is sentenced to imprisonment.*

2. The Role of the Parole Board of Canada (PBC)

Under the *Corrections and Conditional Release Act*, the Parole Board of Canada (PBC) is authorized to investigate royal prerogative of mercy requests for federal offenses.

The PBC's role in clemency cases is to review applications, conduct investigations at the direction of the Public Safety Minister, and make recommendations to the Minister as to whether to grant a clemency request.

In reviewing clemency applications, the PBC uses six guiding principles, which it states provide a fair and equitable process, and ensure that the royal prerogative of mercy is granted only in "very exceptional and truly deserving" cases.

- There must be clear and strong evidence of *substantial injustice or undue hardship,* such as suffering of a mental, physical, and/or financial nature that is *disproportionate* to the nature and the seriousness of the offense and the resulting consequences, and be *more sever* than for other individuals in similar situations.

- Each application is strictly examined on its own merits, solely on the circumstances of the applicant, and may not be considered posthumously.

- The applicant must have exhausted all other avenues available under the *Criminal Code*, or other pertinent legislation, such as through appeals, termination of probation, or a miscarriage of justice.

- The independence of the judiciary shall be respected; therefore, there must be stronger and more specific grounds to recommend action that would interfere with a court's decision.

- A royal prerogative of mercy is intended only for rare cases in which considerations of justice, humanity, and compassion override the normal administration of justice.

- The decision should not, in any way, increase the penalty for the applicant.

To apply for clemency under the royal prerogative of mercy, the official PBC Clemency Application form must be completed, using schedules A and B as a guide:

- Schedule A: http://www.pbc-clcc.gc.ca/prdons/clem-schedule-a-pdf-eng.pdf

- Schedule B: http://www.pbc-clcc.gc.ca/prdons/clem-schedule-b-pdf-eng.pdf

Download Kit

Please enter the URL you see in the box below into your computer web browser to access and download the kit.

www.self-counsel.com/updates/criminalpardon/15kit.htm

The download kit offers online resources to assist in your efforts to obtain a pardon.